THE KNIGHTS TEMPLAR IN SOMERSET

THE
KNIGHTS
TEMPLAR
IN
SOMERSET

JULIET FAITH

The
History
Press

This book is dedicated to my sons Tristan and Tobias, and to the enduring memory of the Knights of the Temple of Solomon

First published 2009

The History Press
The Mill, Brimscombe Port
Stroud, Gloucestershire, GL5 2QG
www.thehistorypress.co.uk

British Library Cataloguing in Publication Data.
A catalogue record for this book is available from the British Library.

ISBN 978 0 7524 5256 2

Typesetting and origination by The History Press
Printed in Great Britain

CONTENTS

ACKNOWLEDGEMENTS

I would like to thank the following people for their help and inspiration with the writing of this book: The Bristol City Museum and Art Gallery, particularly Donnie Hauser, Bruce Williams and Les Good; Dr Clare Ryder; Joe Silmon-Monerri, for his help in tracing the history of the St Maur family; Dr Richard Haddlesey; Anna Kemp; Barry Lane, Barry Watson, Geoff Wilson and Alan Royce. Many thanks also to Clive Wilkins for his help with the research and heroic translations of primary source documents from Latin.

My special thanks go to Mike Flower and Robert (Bob) Williams from Temple Cloud, for their continual help and support over the past three years, and particularly to Bob for his dedicated research, and writing of the chapter about Temple Hydon and Mendip; and not forgetting his wife Barbara, who provided many cups of tea and lunches, whilst listening to non-stop discussion about the Templars!

The photographs in the book have been taken by various friends; these are Alex Meadows; Bob Williams; Mike Flower, and my son Tristan.

Finally, I would like to acknowledge the many people over the years with whom I have discussed the Templars, and who have enlightened me or given me inspiration in one way or another. You know who you are! Thank you.

INTRODUCTION

The Knights Templar first captured my imagination many years ago, when, at the age of fifteen, I visited Somerset with my parents. Whilst there, we visited the Church of St Mary at Templecombe. Inside the church was an unusual and haunting image in the form of a panel painting secured to the church wall. This painting portrays the disembodied head of a bearded man, and is believed by some to be one of four Templar 'icons' reputedly brought to England for safekeeping by Provincial Master of the Templars, William de la More, after the Templars' suppression in France in 1307. Whatever the history behind this strange image, I was left with a sense of mystery and wonder.

Some years later, I became aware of the controversial Turin Shroud, and suggestions by some that the Templecombe panel painting may in fact have been a copy of the face on the Shroud. During the following years the mysterious history of the Knights Templar continued to fascinate me and I became determined to discover more about the Crusades, and in particular the Templars – a remarkable and misunderstood order of warrior monks.

My quest to find traces of the Templar presence in Somerset has led me to some wonderful and beautiful places, magical landscapes and ancient churches, each of which seemed imbued with the very essence of the Templar spirit. It has also allowed me to meet many generous, kind (and sometimes eccentric) people.

The Templar cross atop Cameley Church. (Courtesy of Simon Brighton)

Each chapter contains an overview or 'picture' of the Templars' role and activities at each location, as well as a 'gazetteer' of the sources and documentary evidence that have been drawn upon to create this picture.

I have also included many place names, plans, maps and photographs in this book, my hope being that the reader will feel encouraged to find and explore some of these sites, and perhaps undertake their own quest!

Juliet Faith, 2009

GLOSSARY

Assize of Novel Disseisin – *Action to recover land of which the plaintiff had recently been dispossessed.*

Assize of Mort D'Ancestor – *Action to recover lands/property where plaintiff claimed the defendant had entered on a freehold belonging to him upon the death of one of his relatives.*

Assize of Warranty of Charter – *Action taken by a grantee of land or property, to request the grantor of the land to defend him in his possession of the said land.*

Attaint of Jury – *Action taken to discover if a jury had given a false verdict at trial.*

Carucate – *An area of land that a team of eight oxen could plough in one season.*

Curia Regis Rolls – *Common law records of pleas before the King or his justices.*

Enfeoffed – *To place in possession of land in exchange for services.*

Escheat – *A land law to prevent property being left without an owner if upon the owner's death no will was left. An escheator was a royal official who managed this.*

Final Concord – *The settlement of a legal case, frequently concerning land ownership.*

Judged to be in Mercy – *To be found guilty.*

Messuage – *A house, including outbuildings, garden and orchard.*

Oblate Rolls – *A type of Fine Roll.*

Pannage – *Medieval legal term for turning out pigs into a forest to feed.*

Pertinencie – *An attachment or part of a preceptory or manor but in another area.*

Petty Assizes – *Civil courts established by Henry II in 1156.*

Pipe Rolls – *Financial records held by the English treasury from the twelfth century.*

Preceptory – *An administrative centre or commandery held by the Knights Templar.*

Vill – *A settlement.*

Virgate – *A medieval term for an area of land that two oxen could plough in a season.*

1

A BRIEF HISTORY OF THE TEMPLARS

It is not the literal past that rules us, save, possibly, in a biological sense. It is images of the past. These are often as highly structured and selective as myths. Images and symbolic constructs of the past are imprinted, almost in the manner of genetic information on our sensibility. Each new historical era mirrors itself in the picture and active mythology of its past.

(George Steiner, *In Bluebeard's Castle*, 1971)

Historical background and records

How much is actually known about the Templar holdings in Somerset? In Evelyn Lord's book *The Knights Templar in Britain*, the only Templar properties shown in Somerset are the Preceptory of Templecombe, Lamyatt and Crewkerne. There are, in addition, references to holdings at 'Wileton' and Temple Hydon. There were, however, other Templar possessions in Somerset not accounted for in Evelyn Lord's book, and this book is an attempt to fill in the gaps in what is known about the lands and possessions of the Knights Templar in this historic county.

In England much documentary evidence about the Templars has been accidentally or deliberately destroyed or lost. According to T.W. Parker's book *The Knights Templar in England*, there were full records in existence at New Temple in London at the time of the suppression. It appears that they may have been destroyed at some point during the Peasants' Revolt.

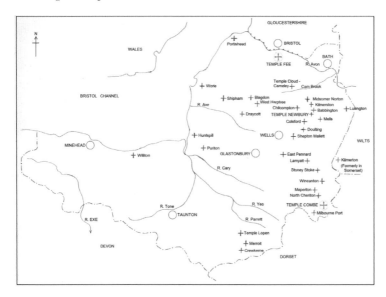

*A map of
Templar holdings
in Somerset.*

The task of putting together the history of the Knights Templar in Somerset has, therefore, been rather like putting together an incomplete jigsaw puzzle. It has been a mixture of searching the Somerset Records Office, the Public Records Office, various libraries and archives; and enlisting the help of other interested and knowledgeable people, not to mention a certain amount of intuition!

The 1185 Inquest, which documents all the land in England held by the Templars at that time, included relatively few land and property holdings in Somerset. During the following decades however, the Templars received large grants of both land and property, increasing their holdings in the county considerably. Not only were the land holdings increased, it also appears that the Templars held mills and manors, and were involved in sheep farming on the Mendips at Temple Hydon.

The map shown above illustrates the extent of the Templar land holdings in Somerset.

The documents that record the properties held by the Order in Somerset until their suppression (and afterwards by the Knights Hospitaller until the dissolution of the monasteries) are held in the Muniment Room at Winchester College. The two manors of Templecombe and Temple Newbury owned between them all the Templar holdings east of the River Parrett, and, according to Evelyn Lord, the preceptory at Bristol 'administered an inland estate that stretched as far as Cornwall'.

The first land in England that was granted to the Templars was that given by King Stephen's wife, Matilda, in 1137. When the Templars were gifted lands and manors, they also inherited all the people that lived and worked on the land.

By 1187, the Templars in Somerset held lands at Temple Fee (Bristol) Portishead, Bishopsworth, Lamyatt, Puriton, Drayton, Templecombe, Merriot, and Crewkerne. In 1201, King John re-affirmed an earlier gift to the Order of Cameley and Temple Cloud. At this time Templecombe was a key preceptory in the South West. Templecombe is situated between the two ports of Bristol and Poole, which would have provided important trade links with Europe.

In the decades that followed, the Templars were granted further lands across Somerset; these appear to lie in clusters along Roman roads or near waterways, giving easier access to scattered villages which would have enabled them to efficiently oversee the running of their estates.

Medieval life

> The Templars have something to do with everything.
> (Umberto Eco, *Foucault's Pendulum*)

The accomplishments of the Knights Templar within the secular life of Britain during the Middle Ages should not be underestimated. A minor industrial revolution was occurring in England during this period and the Templars' contribution towards this was very substantial, primarily due to them being superbly efficient managers of both land and revenue and because they had important trade links with Europe due to their shipping and banking enterprises. It can be shown from surviving records that the lands that they owned and managed were developed to maximum effect, and time and again they substantially increased the value of their assets. The Templars also established the first banking system in Europe, which meant that the medieval traveller or pilgrim could deposit money with the Knights at one preceptory and withdraw it at another, enabling him to travel freely without the fear of being robbed. (A preceptory served as a combination of hostelry, bank, and church and, in the countryside, also as a farm.)

The Knights Templar rapidly established themselves as entrepreneurs in England; developing all the available resources of the English countryside, managing farms and mills, creating markets, and importing and exporting goods across Europe. It has been suggested that the Templars may have acquired special skills in the Holy Land, such as skills in architecture, navigation and medicine (it is believed that they may also have used some crude form of antibiotic). Some believe that the Templars were the inspiration and funding behind the Gothic cathedrals that flowered across Europe during the Middle Ages, which were inspired by Middle Eastern architecture (as can be seen at Garway Church, Herefordshire, and by the concept of sacred geometry). As bankers they would have been able to supply the necessary funds required for the execution of these splendid buildings.

The Knights Templar were granted special status by the English kings which allowed them exemption from export and import duties and also from tax at all bridges and highways as well as markets and fairs across Britain. Unfortunately, this sometimes led to jealousy and resentment amongst others in the locality, which frequently resulted in disputes of one kind or another.

The guidelines for the procedures of running Templar preceptories and manors would have been established at their main headquarters at New Temple in London, and afterwards adopted throughout England, although with the passing of time this structure became a lot less rigid.

A preceptory was an administrative unit generally found in the countryside. As Paul Newman notes in his book *Somerset Villages*, most preceptories were based on monastic models, which would consist of a manor house, refectory, a chapel, and stabling for horses all set around a central courtyard. More usually however, they were sometimes modelled upon secular manors, making them more difficult for archaeologists to define in the landscape than other religious houses.

As the Templars spread across England, acquiring further lands and manors, they emerged as feudal overlords, who managed their estates meticulously, allowing them to raise large amounts of revenue to support the Crusades in the Holy Land.

Many Templar lands and industries would have been worked by laymen and women, but were ultimately overseen by the knights themselves. According to Parker's book *The Knights Templar in England*, the group of manual workers (known as '*les fréres des metiers*') comprising of labourers, servants, craftsmen and artisans, would have thought of themselves as Templars, and would have had a Templar cross on the doors of their dwellings, denoting that they were exempt from tithes. This would also serve to show that they were the Templars' subjects, and fell under their rule. It has been suggested that the Templars often preferred to run their own mills, rather than rely upon outside labour. It is believed that they introduced fulling mills to this country. There were two such mills and a corn mill in the Newbury Temple area.

Each medieval manor consisted of several parts: arable land, meadowland, a common and the village itself, which was always situated near a water supply. A typical manor had an area of wasteland, and would probably have been surrounded by woodland. The entire population of England at this time was under 3 million, and a great deal of the countryside had been undisturbed by man; wild boar, wolves and the King's deer would have roamed the wood land. It was indeed a pastoral, but not an idyllic, existence and would have provided only a very basic level of subsistence for many people.

The cottage homes of the village folk would certainly have been very primitive, usually made of wattle and daub, with a mud floor covered in straw and a roof of thatch with a hole in it so the smoke from the fire could escape. Life for the medieval peasant was often a very precarious existence; apart from ever-present poverty and threat of disease, there was the worry of a bad harvest and continual struggle with the elements and the land; nature was both friend and foe. It is easy to see why the veneration of nature persisted long in medieval society, despite the coming of Christianity. The 'Green Man', for example, is a common image in many early churches, the head disgorging or sprouting foliage as a symbol of fertility and the continuation of life; the 'old gods' were merely incorporated into the new religion.

During this period the inside of churches were painted with brightly coloured pictures that had a meaning and told stories to a congregation, who were largely illiterate. Churches with important patrons would also have contained large amounts of beautiful carved woodwork, which would have been painted and sometimes gilded; sadly this was nearly all destroyed during the Reformation when the beautiful paintings were white washed and carved images destroyed. Templar churches are often carved with 'green men' and other strange (and often pagan) images which were typical of Romanesque art and architecture. Garway Church and Kilpeck in Herefordshire and New Temple in London provide good examples of this style.

Markets and fairs

A medieval village was virtually self-sufficient, with a blacksmith, a carpenter, sometimes a mill and the people growing their own crops, raising their own animals, and preparing their clothing from wool, linen or leather. As was mentioned earlier though, the Templars imported other goods from the continent and the Middle East; some of these were available at markets and fairs in Somerset and throughout England.

Markets in Somerset would have been held weekly, and fairs on particular holy days (which were much more numerous than they are today) and could last up to three days or more; they provided a good source of revenue for the landowner. The English merchants would have traded grain, wool, and the woollen fabric prepared at the local fulling mills, as well as livestock at the fairs, while the European traders would have supplied silks, precious metals, wines, spices and exotic fare.

It was the role of the King to grant the privilege to hold fairs and markets. As the Templars' wealth and power grew, they were granted further rights to hold an increasing number of markets and fairs across the county. By 1185, markets were held at Lamyatt, Puriton, Portishead, Merriot, Crewkerne and Williton. After this date, as more lands were acquired, markets were held in other Somerset towns and villages, allowing for greater exchange of goods and information within the county.

Sadly, despite stunning success in their business, banking and shipping enterprises, once the Holy Land was lost, the situation changed drastically for the Knights Templar.

Lament for the Templars

The trial [of the Templars] was one of the greatest crimes of the Middle Ages.

(W.G. Addison)

One of the aims in writing this book is to highlight the achievements of the Knights Templar in Somerset. It is, however, impossible to write on this subject without speaking of their tragic downfall. Many books have been written on this matter and it will only be dealt with briefly here. It appears that the Knights Templar were treated much more leniently in England than on the continent, especially than in their country of origin, France.

In October 1307 King Philip IV of France issued sealed orders throughout France that were not to be opened until the evening of 12 October. These stated that on the morning of 13 October, every Templar in France, including their Grand Master, Jacques de Molay, was to be arrested.

King Philip was an avaricious man, who had long harboured resentment towards the Templars. He was envious of their wealth and power and he also owed them a great deal of money. It has also been suggested that at one time he had wanted to join the Order, but had been rejected. King Philip had no real authority to arrest the Templars as they were only answerable to the Pope, but although the Pope was reluctant at first, he eventually agreed to support the King. Pope Clement V was both a weak and ailing leader, and as such was willing to go along with the King's plans both for his own benefit and that of the Vatican. The Templars' recent loss of the Holy Land seemed the ideal excuse to strike ... for Philip the timing was perfect.

It should be remembered that the Middle Ages was a time of deep superstition, and a common belief in the power of sorcery and magic. The secrecy which surrounded the Order of the Temple, combined with their power and wealth, all added to the growing speculation that perhaps the Order was indulging in some form of immoral or anti-Christian behaviour. It was believed by many that this was the reason that they had lost the Holy Land. The Templars were accused of similar regressions to the Cathar heretics of the Languedoc in 1209 and were mercilessly tortured for their beliefs, in what became known as the Albigensian Crusade. Amongst the charges against the Knights Templar were; heresy, sodomy, denying Christ, spitting on the cross and worship of idols.

Over the coming months the Templars were interrogated under torture, despite having being given the King's assurance that none would be used. Their former glowing reputation was in tatters; their outstanding achievements forgotten. Ultimately, many were cruelly burnt at the stake, including Jacques de Molay, who suffered years of imprisonment and torture before his death.

King Philip, it appeared, had taken his revenge. It is said that while Jacques de Molay and Geoffrey de Charnay were burning, de Molay called for both Philip IV and the Pope to join him before God. He also protested the innocence of the Order. Within a year both king and pope were dead.

The fate of the Templars in England was not as devastating as that of their French brethren. Initially the English king, Edward II, resisted orders to arrest the Templars, saying that he did not believe the charges against them. It appears that the English public were rather shocked and disbelieving of the accusations against the Order. As far as can be judged, the Templars in England were generally perceived as fair and just landlords. When Edward did finally call for their capture, it was most reluctantly, and the arrests did not come until January 1308.

It has been said that many of the Templars living in England at the time of the suppression were elderly or incapacitated and that is why so few arrests occurred here. Others have suggested (and this is perhaps a more likely scenario) that the delay in the arrests of the English Templars allowed many to escape or simply merge with the secular population. It has been noted by Evelyn Lord that there was an order sent to the Sheriff of Kent to arrest Templars there who were 'wandering about in secular habits committing apostasy'. This was probably the situation throughout most of England. Certainly news would have reached them regarding the fate of the French brothers, allowing time for alternative plans to be made. Whatever the truth behind these suggestions, only 153 Templars were actually seized in England.

In Somerset four knights were arrested at Templecombe and taken to the Tower of London to be interrogated. There seems to be some disagreement as to who these actually were, though Evelyn Lord lists William Burton, John de Ivel, Walter de Rockley and Roger de Wyle. It is thought that William Raven, who was received into the Order at Templecombe before being transferred to Cambridge, was the first to be questioned at the Tower of London. At the trial of Thomas Wothrope he is said to have spoken of a Ricardo Engayne, a Templar fugitive and said to have known him personally.

According to Bishop Drockensfords register of 1315,[1] four Templars, namely Richard Engayne, William de Warwyk, William de Grancombe, and Richard de Colingham were assigned to 'do penance', and live out their days in the Somerset monastic houses of Glastonbury, Taunton, Muchelney and Montacute. 'Maintenance had been paid for these same persons by the Sheriff of Somerset.'

After the suppression of the Templars in 1312, the majority of their possessions passed to the Hospitallers, but there were considerable delays in the Hospitallers obtaining them, and many obstructions were placed in their way. The Templars had held their extensive properties in Somerset under various tenures and of many different lords, who were often in a better position to succeed them than the Hospitallers were. There was an attempt by these noblemen to try and secure the Templar lands for themselves. The King had also seized much of their land and had started to dispose of it as he saw fit. There were royal orders that Templar lands should be delivered to the Hospitallers in 1313 and 1324,[2] but former Templar possessions were still not handed over. Thus in 1332 the Sheriff of Somerset was ordered to sequester all Templar lands that were still withheld and to deliver them to the Hospitallers. It took until 1338 before the efforts of the Hospitallers were rewarded by success.

ENDNOTES

1. *Somerset Record Society* Vol. i, p. 98
2. Perkins (1909), p. 261

2

BRISTOL

In 1145, Robert de Berkeley, Earl of Gloucester, granted lands at Bristol to the Knights Templar. This grant was one of the earliest gifts to the Order of the Temple in England, and enabled them to establish their own small community within the city. This community gradually expanded to become an important location for their shipping, industrial and banking affairs. The district became known as Temple Fee and was situated in the area that is currently occupied by Bristol Temple Meads railway station. Temple Street was originally the main road into the city, and by the late thirteenth century, Bristol was the largest city after London with a population of 10,000. It had also become a key commercial area.

Bishopsworth

Some think that 'Bissopeswrthe' is Bishopsworth in the parish of Bedminster, three miles south-west of Bristol. Bissopeswrthe was a gift of William Fitz John, who held land in Somerset in the twelfth century; it is mentioned in the 1185 Templar Inquest as one of the appurtenances of Bristol.

In Veronica Smith's book *The Street Names of Bristol: Their Origin and Meaning*, she suggests that a field name of 'Templeland' in Bishport Manor is preserved in the 1683 Survey as Templeland Road. The name Bishport derives from the bishop's palace or enclosure; Bishport was the original name for Bishopsworth.

The author at the gates of Temple Church. (Courtesy of Michael Flower)

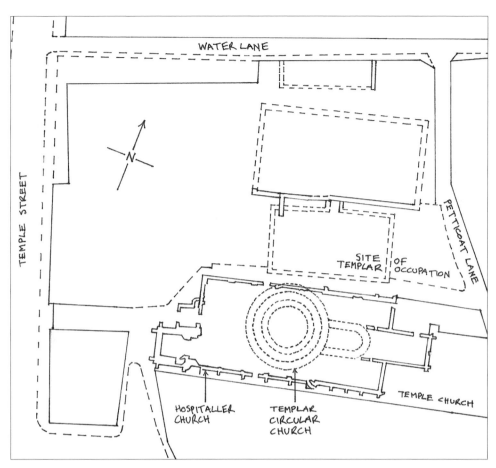

A plan of Temple Church, Bristol. (Barry Watson)

However, Robert Williams, who conducted the research on the Temple Hydon estate, has very convincingly argued recently that Bissopeswrthe is in fact in Mendip, not Bristol, and that Templeland Road was named after Earl 'Temple' of Stowe, who owned the land where Bishport Manor was situated. Earl Temple of Stowe represented mid-Somerset in Parliament in 1892 and assumed the title 'Temple' by Royal licence.

Archaeology

Excavations in 1971 by Les Good on behalf of Bristol City Museum and Art Gallery[1] throw a considerable amount of light on the area between Water Lane and the north of Temple Church. The excavations suggest that

Above & below: *The ruins of Temple Church. (Courtesy of Michael Flower)*

the Templar settlement, or preceptory, would have comprised of a round church and a communal hall, as well as dwellings and other buildings. Documentary evidence informs us that as early as 1185 the Templars had twenty-seven tenants on their fee, including three skinners (suggesting a small tannery); it would appear that the community here was well established by this date.

During earlier excavation work in 1872, foundations were revealed suggesting an oval building. However, in the 1960s, further investigations indicated that it was in fact a rotunda or circular church containing a central nave encircled by an ambulatory and an apsidal chancel; this was the original Templar church. The rotunda was a design frequently adopted by the Templars and was probably modelled on the Temple in Jerusalem. However, not all Templar churches were round and there is some evidence to suggest that over time the circular design was changed to the more frequently used rectangular design. An example of this is to be seen at Garway Church in Herefordshire, where part of the old circular church is revealed lying beneath the later rectangular building.

It is believed that the Bristol rotunda was constructed by 1147, making it one of the earliest of its kind in England. The ground plan of this early building can still be seen amidst the ruined tower and aisled nave of a

The ruins of Hospitaller Church. (Courtesy of Michael Flower)

Looking towards the tower of Temple Church. (Courtesy of Michael Flower)

later fourteenth-century church. This later church has a curious leaning perpendicular tower, due to the foundations sinking into the marshy ground very early on in its construction.

Further excavations by Les Good and team during 1971 and 1972 revealed that the probable preceptory hall of the Templar period was replaced by a larger building to the north, and the former courtyard had been replaced by a garden during the Hospitaller occupation of the area. A ditch and red-mortared wall were also discovered, which may have formed part of the northern boundary of the precinct and could have been of either the Templar or Hospitaller period. The hall was 25m long by 13–14m wide and, though very little of it still remains, evidence suggests that it had a superstructure of wood and a shingle roof.

Pottery shards relating to the Templar era were found in the garden area, some of which were wine jars; these green-glazed jars were identified as coming from south-west France. This type of pottery only started arriving at the port of Bristol from the middle of the thirteenth century, but became one of the most common imports into medieval Bristol.

The *Bristol and Avon Archaeological Journal* of 2007, mentions recent excavations at Finzal's Reach, Temple parish, where a very interesting artefact was found. This was the wooden bridge of a medieval plucked, string instrument known as a rebec. It is believed to have been brought

The leaning tower of Temple Church. (Courtesy of Michael Flower)

back from the Middle East by home-coming crusaders. The rubebe, as it was originally known in the Arab world, was a pear-shaped three-stringed instrument, played under the chin with a bow, like a violin. It was in common use throughout the Byzantine Empire, and spread rapidly through Europe during the eleventh century. It is indeed a romantic thought to imagine a war-weary Templar returning home with such an instrument, presumably listened to and enjoyed in the Holy Land, as a souvenir from his quest and a taste of another world!

The weaving industry in Bristol

Architectural evidence suggests that some time before 1400 the 'Weavers Chapel' was added to the structure of Temple Church, and although no documentary evidence exists to support this, the tracery windows are suggestive of a thirteenth-century date. The Templars were instrumental in the expansion of the weaving industry in England during the Middle Ages and the Bristol area in particular became renowned for its textile industry, and a Guild of Weavers was established there.

During excavations of 1974, evidence of 'tenter' frames were found at Tucker Street in the Temple area of the city, and there is also the possibility that 'fulling' took place on the site, as a stone-lined cistern trough for foot fulling was also discovered nearby. (The following chapter describes the cloth-making process in more detail).

It would appear however, that it was predominantly the process of dyeing cloth which was carried out in the Temple area from the thirteenth century onwards. There is archaeological evidence to support this, with the discovery of the remains of a dye-works. Madder dye (red) was imported from the Low Countries throughout the medieval period, and woad plants (blue) were imported from Bordeaux. Alum, which was used to 'fix' the colours, came from ports in the Mediterranean.

Shipping

Bristol was the second most important port in Britain after London as far as the Templars were concerned; it was not only a vital port for the import of French goods and wine from Gascony,[2] but for the shipment of wool, textiles, and other goods to Europe and the East. Bristol would also have been a key port for the departure of knights and horses to the Holy Land, and pilgrims to various sites of pilgrimage in Europe and the East. As one

The River Avon, Temple, Bristol. (Courtesy of Michael Flower)

of the foremost Templar roles was to guard pilgrims on crusade, travellers would have enjoyed rest and refreshment at Templar hostelries in Bristol before embarking on their arduous journey overseas.

The Templars constructed a stone bridge over the River Avon and the river was first dammed and then diverted through the Portwall Ditch. The diversion of the river made access for shipping much easier. The Templars also joined with the Parish of Redcliffe to build the Portwall, which was the outer defensive wall of the city, south of the river. The Portwall is now almost completely gone or hidden underground, save for a small section that was discovered in 1980, which visitors to Bristol may view today, near Temple Quay. Also found were the suggested remains of a tower, now buried beneath a building at Harratz Place, Temple. Tolls were charged at the gates to traders coming in and out of the city. The fees charged paid for the upkeep of the wall. An early plan of the city by Georgius Hoefnagle (1581) shows six towers on the wall, while a later plan by Jacobus Millerd (1673) depicts eight round towers and two main gates.[3]

In Julian Lea-Jones' book *Bristol Curiosities*, he notes that in the 1980s a local history group discovered evidence of a small creek or dock at the end of Water Lane where the Templar ships were probably once moored. It appears that two Templar ships, *Le Buzard*, a merchant ship, and *La Templere*, a galley, were both registered at Bristol.

Disputes

It appears from documentary accounts that the Bristol Templars sometimes became embroiled in disputes with their neighbours. In 1243, two horses tied to a pillar in one of the streets in Temple Fee broke their halters, and the pillar fell and crushed a boy to death. The 'bailiffs and coroners' of Redcliffe found the Templars were answerable to the price of 10s for the horses, and 2s for the pillar. The Templars would not appear in court; neither would they let the Bristol bailiff enter their land. They did however pay the 12s fine that they owed.

In 1221, the Templars of Redcliffe were summoned to answer to the Redcliffe burgesses, but they did not appear, and were held to be in mercy. It is documented that the Templars claimed they were only answerable to themselves and not to anyone else 'either in Bristol or the county of Somerset, at the will of the King'. There is no surviving record of the judgement, if indeed there was any, passed upon them.

Various other incidents (listed in the gazetteer at the end of the chapter) seem to indicate that perhaps the Templars of Bristol were not the easiest

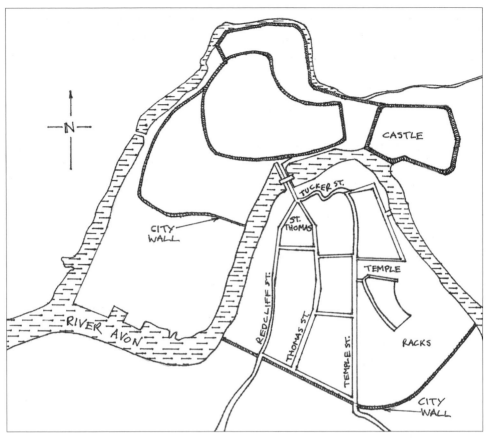

A plan showing the Portwall. (Barry Watson)

Harratz Place, former site of Harratz Tower, Portwall. (Courtesy of Michael Flower)

people to have as neighbours. The aforementioned example seems to indicate that the Templars believed themselves to be beyond reproach, and perhaps this accounts for them sometimes being described as 'proud' and 'haughty'!

Administration in the South West

Bristol in the early Middle Ages was evidently a thriving and important hub of Templar industry, and probably by 1185 the Bristol preceptory was the original administrative centre for the whole of the South West. However, many of the appurtenances in South West England which were listed in the 1185 Templar Inquest as being members of the Bristol preceptory would have been quite difficult to oversee from Bristol itself.

The 1185 Inquest shows Templecombe as a pertinence of Bristol. At some point however Templecombe itself became a preceptory, and then Bristol became a dependency on Templecombe. Why did the Templars move their main administrative centre in the South West from Bristol to Templecombe, seemingly a backwater?

Templecombe was located very close to the route shown on the medieval 'Gough Map' (which is named after an antiquarian, Richard Gough, who made a study of it in 1780). The original purpose of this map is unknown, though it is believed to be an official government compilation of about 1360 and shows a national road system radiating from London. The roads shown are clearly very important routes.[4]

The route which passes Templecombe (commonly referred to as Hindle's M1), ran westward from London, through Kingston, Cobham, Guildford, Farnham, Alton, Alresford, Winchester, Salisbury, Shaftesbury, Crewkerne, Chard, Honiton, Exeter, Okehampton, Launceston, Camelford, Bodmin and St Column to St Ives. (It is notable that the map does not show all important places or roads, thus Plymouth, another very important town in the South West (which Hindle ranks as the fifth largest town in the country in 1330s), is not shown on the Gough map.) For much of its course Hindle's M1 corresponds with the route known in Anglo-Saxon times as London Way, which ran from London, through Guildford to Ilchester (*see Atlas of Anglo-Saxon England*). At the town of Chard the route of the Gough Map is intersected by the Fosse way. (The Fosse way was another very important medieval (formerly Roman) road, and one of the royal roads of England.) Thus, logistically, this road would have been very important to the Templars, and Templecombe would therefore have been better placed than Bristol to administer their scattered holdings in the South West, and to maintain a good connection to London.

Gazetteer

By the late thirteenth and early fourteenth centuries, Bristol was the second largest city in England after London, with a population in excess of 10,000. (Hindle lists Bristol as the third largest town in England in the 1330s.) Bristol was a convenient crossing point on the River Avon and had developed into a trading centre by the ninth century. By 1200, it was a walled city with a royal castle and had already begun to spread beyond its walls.

The parish of St Mary Redcliffe was in existence by 1158. This settlement was situated in the Berkeley fee and was intended to become a trading rival to Bristol. Redcliffe and Bristol were taxed separately until they realised that it would be more profitable if they were united and could work together in common interest.

Some time before 1147, the Templars were given land at Redcliffe by Robert, Earl of Gloucester, and the Templar church was built before the death of Robert in 1147. An illustration in *History4u – Bristol Historical Research-Temple Local History Group, about Temple Fee* shows a reconstruction of the Temple Fee about 1150 and depicts 'The Templars' Hospice and adjacent round church' and also two Templar ships moored at their dock on the River Avon.

The Templars were influential in projects on the River Avon which helped to improve access to the port for shipping. Their motivation for this was probably that Bristol, along with Dover, was one of the main points of entry for Gascon wine and victuals sent from their French preceptories. From evidence in the Patent Rolls the indications are that this was their own use and not for resale![5]

Before 1147: Robert, Earl of Gloucester, illegitimate son of Henry I, had given the Templars an estate (*terra*), which was the origin of the later Templar division of the city that was to become known as the 'Templar Fee' in the sixteenth century. The parishes of St Mary Redcliffe and St Thomas were formerly treated as part of Somerset, not Gloucestershire, although there was some doubt on the subject even in the thirteenth century.[6] The grant consisted of the eastern part of the marsh. For a time, this estate became the administrative centre for the Templar lands in the South West.[7]

1396–7 Calendar:

> Bristoll, no 106 – Quitclaim of the Abbot of St Augustine Bristol and the convent of the same place of 4s 1d yearly rent.[8]

1185 Templar Inquest: The donation as entered in the Inquest amounted to about '28 messuages' and '2 terre' with a gross rental of £2 9s 4d. Bristol Preceptory was listed as the fiscal centre of a wide circumference of outlying lands in Gloucestershire, Somerset, Dorset, Devon and Cornwall, with a special roll (*rotulus*) for the city and its appurtenances, three special '*Summe*', for city, appurtenances and mills and a general '*Summa tocius rotuli*'.[9]

Appurtenances of Bristol: The identification of the Appurtenances of Bristol is not easy as they extend into five counties and the entries in the Inquest pass from one county to another with no apparent reason. The solution to the tangle is probably to be found in the feudal records of the great Somerset and Devonshire honours: Dunster, Bampton, Bradninch, Barnstaple, Totnes and Plympton but, as Lees stated, 'until this field of research has been more thoroughly explored the exact location of the Templars' lands in the west of England must remain largely a matter of guesswork'.[10]

In all, the Templars received nearly £38 annually from the Bristol Pertinencie, and their mills at Broad Clyst in Devon, Launceston in Cornwall and Lacock in Wiltshire brought in a further 25s a year. All of these rents were paid in money – no labour services were entered on the Bristol roll – and, as Lees states, 'it may perhaps be inferred that the wide dispersion of small rural properties, paying dues to a distant urban centre, which in turn was responsible to London, tended to spread the use of money exchange and to commercialize land tenure and feudal service'.[11]

Crukes (Crewkerne)	1 mark rent
Merieth (Merriott)	1 virgate
Piritonam (Puriton)	half a virgate
Menedepe (at Mendip?)	a holding worth half a mark
Draintune (Drayton, probably near Langport)	12d rent (?)
Portisheued (Portishead)	1 virgate
Lamiete (Lamyatt)	1 messuage
Holeweie (? Somerset or Dorset)	1 virgate
Cumbam (Temple Combe)	all the vill of Cumba
Bissopeswrthe (Bishopsworth, probably in Bedminster, Bristol)	60 acres
Wiletune (Williton)	all the vill of Williton

1221: The Templars of Bristol seem to have been troublesome people, as illustrated by a reference in the Rolls of the Gloucestershire Eyre:

The Templars in Redcliffe were summoned to answer with the burgesses of that place. They did not come on the first day and were held to be in mercy. They appear to have claimed to answer by themselves and not with the burgesses, although it was shown that they were accustomed to answer with others and that they ought to do so, either in Bristol or the county of Somerset, at the will of the King. They replied that they would not answer with the others of Redcliffe outside the county of Somerset, but admitted that when the justices were in Somerset, they had refused to answer.

Maitland says that this must have been in 1218–19 although there does not seem to be a record of that eyre.[12]

1226: On 22 July the Fine Rolls of Henry III record the following:

Arnold son of Hamo and John of Cardiff, burgesses of Bristol, give the King four tuns of wine so that they might have quit 50 of their cloths seized at the fair of Holland by the King's order, because they were not of the correct breadth according to the assize of cloths made in the realm. Order to William de Haverhill and William le Taillur to cause them to have those cloths. Alan, Master of the Knights of the Temple, is their pledge for the aforesaid tuns of wine.[13]

1238: In May a mandate was sent by the King to the bailiffs of Bristol telling them to supply good barrels and carts to 'John de Plessis, Brother Robert the Templar and a Hospitaller', so that they could transport the King's revenues from the tax of the thirtieth to the New Temple in London.[14]

1243: Two horses tied to the pillory in the street of the Templars (in *vico qui est Templariorum*) broke their halters; the pillory fell and crushed a young boy to death. The horses were in the custody of the Templars. The bailiffs and coroners of 'la Radeclive' valued the horses at 10s and the price of the pillory at 2s and called the Templars to answer for both. However, the Templars did not come to answer for anything and they would not allow any bailiff of Bristol to enter their land to make any attachment. There was no record of a judgement if any, passed on them for not appearing in court, but there was a marginal note showing that they did pay the 12s to the sheriff and that this represented the deodand.[15] (Deodand was an animal or inanimate object which contributed to the death of someone who had reached the age of discretion and was believed to share the guilt of their death. The object or its value was forfeited to the Crown, which applied it for charitable purposes.)

1269: It is recorded that pleas were held before Adam de Greinvill in the Church of the Holy Cross of the Temple on 16 August 1269:

> Geoffrey Dune who brought an Assize of Novel Disseisin against Richard le Draper regarding a tenement in the suburbs of Bristol was not to proceed, so Dune and his pledges for prosecution were in mercy. The pledges were Walter Page and William Humfray.[16]

1299: A plaque attached to the wall of the chapel in the nineteenth century referred to the granting of the chapel (St Catherine's, Temple Church) for the use of the Company of Weavers. There is no original documentation to support this.[17]

Before 1300: Architectural evidence, provided by the geometrical tracery patterns of the windows, suggests that major alterations were made to Temple Church shortly before 1300, when a rectangular chancel replaced the apse with a chapel to the north. If this dating were correct, this would have been when the church was acquired by the Hospitallers after the suppression of the Templars.[18]

1334–5: The Buckland Cartulary contains the following entry:

> Inquisition at Somerton, taken before Ralph de Middelneye escheator of the King in Somerset, Dorset, Cornwall and Devon, of the manors, land and tenements of the Hospital of St John of Jerusalem in England, included those formerly belonging to the Knights Templar. They held in Demesne Templestret in Bristol, which street formerly belonged to the Templars.[19]

1335: A report was made by the Bishop of Bath and Wells to the King regarding all the churches and advowsons and pensions which the Prior and Brethren possessed in the diocese of Bath and Wells; they only had one – the Church of the Temple at Bristol – from which they drew 2 marks a year 'by the hand of the vicar'.[20]

1338: Hospitaller Survey:[21]

a small appropriated church	4 marks
fixed rents per annum	2½ marks
pleas and perquisites of the court	1 mark

1339: A return of Bishop Ralph de Salopia to the King concerning possessions belonging to the Order of St John of Jerusalem in the diocese of Bath and Wells states that the Order had appropriated the Temple Church from which they are paid 100s a year by the vicar of that church 'for the time being'.[22]

Because the Hospitallers owned the former Temple fee, the area retained a degree of independence of Bristol, even though it lay within the bounds of the town, and was incorporated into the County of Bristol by Edward III's charter of 1373.

ENDNOTES

1. Bristol and Avon Archaeological Society Excavation at Water Lane, by Temple Church, Bristol, 1971
2. Lord, E., *The Knights Templar in Britain* (Longman, 2002), p. 116
3. These plans are held at the Bristol City Museum, and further information of the excavations can be found in Williams, B., 'Excavations in the Medieval Suburbs of Bristol', *BARAS*
4. Hindle (1989), pp. 17–20
5. Lord (2002), pp. 154, 156
6. Lees, Beatrice A., *Records of the Templars in England in the Twelfth Century Inquest of 1185* (London 1935), p. cxxxi
7. Good, G.L., *Excavation at Water Lane, by Temple Church Bristol 1971* (Published by Bristol and Avon Archaeology, 1992), p. 2
8. *Somerset and Dorset Notes and Queries* Vol. xxi p. 92
9. Lees (1935), pp. cxxxi–cxxxii
10. ibid, p. cxxxii
11. ibid, p. cxxxv
12. *SRS* Vol. xi note, p. 239
13. Fine Rolls Henry III Vol. 10, p. 228
14. Cal Librate Rolls 1226–40, pp. 230, 309 (in Lord p. 222)
15. *SRS* Vol. xi p. 239
16. ibid Vol. xxxvi p. 106
17. Good (1992), p. 4
18. ibid, p. 4
19. Buckland Cartulary *SRS* Vol. xxv (1909) p. 111
20. Hugo, 'Mynchin Buckland Priory and Preceptory', *Somerset Archaeological and Natural History Society* Vol. 10 (ii) (1860), pp. 47–9
21. *Knights Hospitallers in England* Camden Society p. 184
22. Hugo (1860), p. 56

3

TEMPLECOMBE

Today, the village of Templecombe would be barely recognisable to the Knights Templar. With an Inter City station and modern housing, it is hard to imagine that it was once the site of their main preceptory in the South West. Few of the old buildings still survive, as the village was devastated at the time of the Second World War. However, the history of the village is a long and fascinating one. Templecombe originally formed two separate manors; Temple Combe or Combe Templar was one of the two estates in Combe divided by a valley.

Abbas Combe

Abbas Combe was the older of the two manors and belonged to the Abbey at Shaftsbury, which was then the most important nunnery in England. Shaftesbury Abbey had been founded by King Alfred in AD 888, and his daughter Aethelgifu, his third surviving child, was the first abbess. It is believed that Aethelgifu was probably only a teenager when she became Abbess of Shaftesbury and the King's decision to make her a nun was probably for political reasons (to ensure that she would never produce a son and thus 'dilute' the royal blood). It would appear from Alfred's biographer, Asser, that from an early age Aethelgifu was destined for a religious life. It is believed that she had been brought up in one of the mixed monastic houses of Wessex. The founding of Shaftesbury Abbey as a monastic house for nuns alone was a new departure and represented the first of its kind in England.

King Alfred probably founded Shaftesbury Abbey to thank God for his kingdom and victories and also because he believed that it would help to secure his place in heaven (this was a common idea in the medieval period).

Temple Combe

Before 1066 Combe was held by Earl Leofwine, half-brother of King Harold. After the Battle of Hastings, in 1086, William the Conqueror gave Combe to his half-brother and fellow soldier, Odo Bishop of Bayeux and his tenant Samson. Odo in turn gave it to his son Serlo Fitz Odo. It is also known that land at Milborne Port was held by the Bishop of Bayeux and was a 'detachment' of Combe; it was called 'Thorent' and is today represented by Thorent Field and Thorent Hill. The Templars acquired this land in Milborne Port with the grant of Combe. The Close Rolls of 1330–3 mention that 'The town bailiff occupied former Templar property, consisting of two messuages in the town'.

There is some confusion as to who actually granted Combe to the Knights Templar. William Martell, the King's Butler, is recorded as having gifted the land to the Order before 1136. This is documented in 'The Inquest of the Templar Lands in Somerset and Dorset' in the National Archives. However, according to 'The 1185 Inquest' (which was a survey of all Templar lands in England at that date), Serlo Fitz Odo gifted them Combe. Finally, according to Feudal Aids, Combe was granted to the Templars by King Henry II.

After the Templars acquired Combe, it became known as Templecombe. The preceptory buildings were situated along the north-south route through the parish, while the Templar lands were situated on the south side of the stream at Combe. A map of 1838 shows the two medieval animal pounds, one belonging to the abbey, the other to the Knights. Separate courts were recorded for the manors of Abbas Combe and Temple Combe. Along with Bristol Temple fee (which is now the area around Templemeads station), Templecombe is probably the best-known site of Templar occupation in the South West of England.

The Templars held Combe from an early date, and at sometime before the Suppression, Templecombe, rather than Bristol, became the main preceptory for the management of the Templar estates in the South West of England.

Arrest and loss

In 1308, the Knights Templar at Templecombe were arrested and taken to the nearest royal castle to be interrogated; this was Sherborne Castle in Dorset. Our translation of the 1308 documents show that only three brothers were arrested at Templecombe; these were John de Iveleah, Reginald de Wyk (or Wykes) and William de Burton. (Alternatively, Evelyn Lord gives them as John de Ivel, William Burton, Roger de Wyle and Walter de Rockley, although it is probable that Walter de Rockley was from Rockley in Wiltshire, not Templecombe.) William Raven was also arrested; he had originally been received into the Order at Templecombe, before being transferred to Cambridge. Eventually all these men were taken to the Tower of London and William Raven was the first to be questioned there.

On 6 October 1308, there was an order to John de Crumbwell, constable of the Tower of London, to deliver all the Templars in the Tower to the inquisitors and prelates appointed to enquire concerning their Order, either singly or in a body according to their instructions. He was also to imprison the Templars in the Tower when and as often as the prelates requested him to. The inquisitors were 'to do what they shall think with the bodies of the Templars according to ecclesiastical law'.

In 1332, Temple Combe Manor was given to the Knights Hospitaller, who held it until the dissolution; at that time the manor is said to have consisted of a capital messuage with a garden, two dovecotes, 368 acres and a small area of wood. It seems that after the arrest of the Templars, and before the Hospitallers acquired the manor, the wood was decimated by whoever occupied the manor. This appears to be a common theme in Somerset. The 1338 Survey speaks of 'ruined messuages' at Long Load and Lopen, and 'exhausted land' at Westcombeland. It would appear that many saw the arrest of the Templars as an opportunity to loot and pillage their land and property, and order was not restored until the new Lords of the Manor were installed.

Bruton Priory

Bruton Priory, a few miles from Templecombe, was founded in 1240 by William de Bohun. The Bruton Cartulary of 1240 tells us that Knights Templar from Templecombe were buried at the priory and that the brothers of Templecombe were paid 3s annually to pray 'for the souls of their brethren' who were buried there. Quite why there were Templars buried

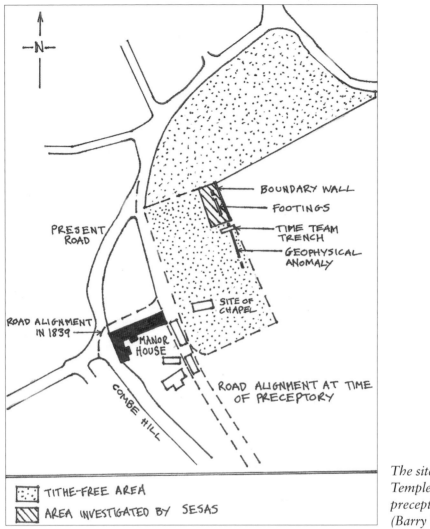

—N—

BOUNDARY WALL
FOOTINGS
TIME TEAM TRENCH
GEOPHYSICAL ANOMALY

PRESENT ROAD

SITE OF CHAPEL

ROAD ALIGNMENT IN 1839

MANOR HOUSE

COMBE HILL

ROAD ALIGNMENT AT TIME OF PRECEPTORY

TITHE-FREE AREA
AREA INVESTIGATED BY SESAS

The site of the Templecombe preceptory. (Barry Watson)

at Bruton rather than Templecombe is unclear. One possibility is that there was a hospital of some kind at Bruton, and elderly or infirm Templars were being looked after there. Certainly by 1291 a hospital dedicated to St Catherine was founded in the town, which by the late fourteenth century was providing for the poor, lepers and other sick and infirm people. It is quite likely therefore that there was some form of earlier infirmary in the town.

Unfortunately, no manorial records survive to show us how the canons of Bruton administered their priory, so the exact reason that Templars were buried there will probably remain a mystery.

The preceptory

The main function of the Templecombe preceptory was as an administrative centre for Templar lands in the South West and Cornwall. T.W. Parker suggests that, apart from administrative functions, preceptories would have served as recruitment centres for the Order. Others believe that Templecombe would have served as a training ground for both men and horses, to enable them to practice and maintain their fighting skills before making a Crusade. It was here that men and horses from the South West would have made spiritual and physical preparations before embarking on their arduous journey overseas to realise their role as defenders of the faith in the Holy Land and protectors of pilgrims on their journey to various shrines across Europe and the Middle East.

Immediately prior to the dissolution of the Order, at the time of the arrests, only a preceptor, two brothers and their servants occupied the main house, or 'capital messuage'. It is, however, very likely that there were a greater number occupying the house in former years. Evelyn Lord suggests that 'a group of brothers' would have lived in a preceptory.

The Chaplain of the Order would have had his own house. Chaplains were not usually Templars themselves, but were affiliated with the Order. The small, simple chapel at Templecombe would have been where the daily services and rituals would have taken place. The Templars followed the Rule laid down by the Cistercian St Bernard; their vow was 'Poverty, Chastity and Obedience'.

The preceptory would also have comprised of a hall, kitchen, refectory, dairy and brew house, as well as stabling for the horses and other animals. Skilled blacksmiths and farriers would have worked in the smithy, and grooms and squires would have attended to the well-being of both horse and rider.

A hostelry of some kind would have existed at Templecombe, in common with other Templar preceptories. Many visitors, both ecclesiastical and secular, would have sought food and rest here, as it was strategically well placed for travellers. There has been suggestion that the former Blue Boar Inn, which is now a private house named Lion Gate, could have been such a hostelry. Audrey Dymock-Herdsman (a local historian) recalled that until the 1960s the interior of the property consisted of 'a central area with two projecting arms, partly enclosing a yard or forecourt', she also noted that there were some very ancient beams within.

In Helen Nicholson's book *Knight Templar*, she explains that the Templar= Rule does not give any particular instruction as to how the knights should be trained in combat, although any new knights joining the Order would be expected to already be accomplished warriors, as would their sergeants. It is known from the Templar Rule that it was acceptable for them to joust and race their horses, but they were forbidden to throw their lances, because this activity held a high risk of very serious injury. We also know that the knights were expected to march together, and Helen Nicholson comments that Templar warriors charged together in a close knit 'eschielle' in such a way as to break through the Muslim battle lines, thus scattering the enemy. It seems that this 'charge' terrified the Muslim forces. Templars became known for moving as one body in battle, and fighting to the death; as such they would have presented a formidable adversary. This skill of moving together as one in a disciplined charge must have been taught to the knights after they joined the Order because, as Nicholson observes, it was not the practice for western knights to charge in such a manner, and would have taken a considerable amount of skill. Again, unfortunately, the Rule is silent on this.

It would appear that the Templars were mostly mounted fighters not foot soldiers, and their main weapon was the sword, although they would have been familiar with the crossbow, lance, the mace and other medieval weaponry.

Documentary evidence tells us that each knight had three horses and each sergeant had one, though the number of knights residing at Templecombe would have varied greatly.

Documentary evidence

Documentary evidence suggests that the Templecombe preceptory comprised over 400 acres and there has been some archaeological work carried out which provides us with clues about the extent of the preceptory site, and its location.

In 1996, the *Time Team* television series carried out a three-day 'dig' at Templecombe. The team were working on a long-held assumption that the present manor house was built on earlier foundations and it was understood these might have originally formed part of the preceptory buildings. Disappointingly, it was discovered that no medieval masonry or early re-used stone survives in the seventeenth-century manor house.

Adjoining the manor house can be found a series of out buildings where the present owner had uncovered an area of cobblestones on the floor. There is also to be found an enormous fireplace, thought to be the largest in the South West, that would have probably served as a kitchen range. Unfortunately, the beams over the fireplace were made of elm, which is unsuitable for dendrochronological dating. Above these beams, however, was an oak beam, from which a sample was taken. Disappointingly, this date proved to be about 1610+, much later than the period of Templar occupation. It may of course be possible that the oak beam was added to the building at a later time, when the house underwent alterations, though as yet there is no evidence either way. It is thought now that the fireplace was probably associated with the later, Hospitaller refectory.

Temple Combe Manor House and modern Manor Farm

As the dig progressed, and little evidence of Templar occupation was emerging, the team decided that they were searching in the wrong location. Because the focus had been on the manor house, they had overlooked the fact that Templar lands were usually tithe free. They therefore consulted the old tithe maps to find other areas where the Templar buildings might be located. Their new trenches produced evidence of what they believed to be the likely heart of the preceptory site. It appears therefore that the lands lay to the north of the Manor Farm, not the south as was previously believed. A boundary wall was uncovered to the north of the modern Manor Farm; this was of thirteenth-century origin and probably represented part of the boundary wall of the preceptory. This precinct would be where most of the day-to-day running of a preceptory manor and farm took place. Although the enclave was surrounded by a wall, further earthworks recorded outside this wall may also represent part of the preceptory complex. The excavations carried out by *Time Team* were not able to establish an internal ground plan for the preceptory.

Remnants of Wessex Style floor tiles were discovered, which were of typical medieval style. About ten different designs were identified, and were red in colour with creamy white motifs. The designs included heraldic images and Catherine wheels. Further remnants included green border tiles, which may have edged the preceptory floor. These finds indicated elaborately tiled floors within some areas of the excavation site and suggest a building(s) of a certain wealth and status.

This archaeological evidence is strengthened by the fact that when the Knights Hospitaller took possession of the estate in around 1338 after the Templar suppression, it was worth £106 13s, making it the ninth wealthiest Templar estate in the country.

Further excavations carried out as a 'rescue dig' in 1996 by South East Somerset Archaeological and Natural History Society (SESAHS) has added to our knowledge of this site. They identified a line of large-faced stones away from the chapel remains, which they believe suggested a

The manor house, Templecombe. (Courtesy of Alex Meadows)

A side view of the manor house. (Courtesy of Alex Meadows)

The remains of the Templar chapel. (Courtesy of Alex Meadows)

barn/workshop or kitchen. Shards of medieval pottery and animal bone, including deer and fish, were found. Also identified was a probable medieval road alignment that 'lay along the western edge of the preceptory, following the edge of the tithe free land'.

The remains of walls at the site of the former Templar chapel are today to be found serving as a vegetable plot in the grounds of the present-day Manor Farm. In a nineteenth-century photograph in *Somerset and Dorset Notes and Queries* the carved stone of the chapel windows can be seen still in place. Manor Farm farmhouse itself is a modern building, beyond which the 'Sites and Monuments Record' mention earthworks that could have been fishponds and may have been associated with the preceptory, as fishponds indicate a manorial complex. Today it is covered by a housing development. The SESAHS finds are housed at Taunton Museum, along with a full report of their findings.

A badge

In 1886, an armorial badge was discovered during work on some cottages not far from the preceptory buildings. The badge shows two lions passant on a background that was once red but has turned green due to oxidisation. It was discovered amongst remains of burnt buildings and animal bones, which included sheep, dog, horse, cow and also boars' tusks. It has been suggested that the badge is the emblem of a family known as Le Strange, and is of fourteenth- or fifteenth-century date.

The panel painting

In St Mary's Church at Templecombe hangs a strange and haunting image of a man's head, which appears to have an equally mysterious history! It is a painting of the head of a man with long hair and a forked beard, and is cut off at the neck. The image, which some believe to be Christ, has no halo.

The head was discovered by accident sometime during the Second World War. It was found in an outhouse attached to a cottage at 3 West Court. Audrey Dymock-Herdsman suggested that the cottage may have been the Templars' chaplain's house. This is because it was apparently once named the Old Rectory, and, as it is nowhere near St Mary's Church (which is situated in the former Abbas Combe), it may well be associated with Templar Chapel, which it was close to. One of the arguments against this idea is that the cottage is situated outside the wall of the former preceptory boundary. However, this may or may not have made a difference to where the priest lived. The cottage has been so altered over the years that it is difficult to say with any certainty how it would have originally looked.

Some years ago, Ian Wilson, author of several books about the Shroud of Turin, was able to speak with Mrs Molly Drew, who lived in the cottage and had found the painting. She gave him an account of the discovery:

On going into the outhouse she noticed plaster on the floor. Looking up, she saw a face looking down at her! After trying to remove more plaster, she had to enlist the help of workmen, as the panel was heavy and had been fixed very securely into the ceiling, suggesting that it had been deliberately concealed.

Mrs Drew described the image as originally being 'very brightly coloured'. Unfortunately, a local vicar decided to clean the painting in the bath, with Vim; this had dire consequences! Much of the bright-coloured paint that Mrs Drew had seen was washed away. The colours were described as being bright red, blue and green.

In 1955, Eve Baker, a conservator from London (ARCA), was employed to preserve and stabilise the painting, to prevent it from further damage and decay. Whilst conserving the image she found the remnants of ten

St Mary's Church, Templecombe. (Courtesy of Alex Meadows)

or so gold stars on the panel, she was unable to save them completely, although in special lighting conditions it is possible for them to be seen. She also noted that the bright blue that Mrs Drew had seen on first removal of the image was azurite, which is difficult to bind and can be removed easily. Further restoration work in the 1980s by Anna Hulbert uncovered microscopic amounts of scarlet (vermillion) and bright green (verdigris). The vivid image that Molly Drew first saw must have been very different from the one hanging in the church today.

The 'outhouse'

The 'outhouse' where the painting was discovered was demolished many years ago, so its original purpose will remain unknown. One strange aspect of the building was that it had no windows, merely a porthole 18in across. Mrs Drew said that the building was big enough to hold about ten people, and the floor was earth. Until the 1980s the porthole itself survived, set in a garden wall between two cottages. Sadly it has been removed in recent times, and is apparently in the hands of a local collector. The porthole may or may not have had a direct relationship

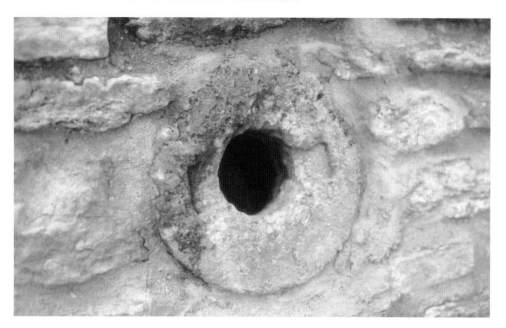

The 'porthole'. (Courtesy of Ian Wilson)

with the panel painting; we can only speculate. It has been suggested that it formed some important function as a peephole to view the painting, or that the outhouse itself was some form of chapel, whereby knights about to leave for the Holy Land could contemplate the image of the Lord, before leaving on their mission.

When one remembers the trials of the Templars, and the accusations of 'worshipping an idol in the form of a head', it is tempting to think that perhaps this is one of these very 'idols', securely hidden from the eyes of the inquisitors; a treasure that they were determined should not be found and destroyed. This idea will be examined further in the final chapter of the book. The panel painting has been carbon 14 dated, and produced a date of around AD 1280. This date puts it firmly within the time of the Knights Templar occupation of Templecombe.

It is believed that the Templars bought, sold and had possession of some very important relics. It has been suggested that perhaps the panel painting is a copy of the face on the Shroud of Turin, which many believe they may have smuggled out of Constantinople after the destruction of the city by Crusaders at the time of the fourth crusade. The trade in relics reached incredible heights during the Middle Ages, with most churches, abbeys and cathedrals having a relic, or relics of saints. The more important the saint, the more valuable the relic, and relics claiming to have a connection to Jesus

The Templecombe panel painting. (Courtesy of Alex Meadows)

were the most prized of all. In his book *Somerset Villages*, Paul Newman suggests that the Templars 'regarded it as their task to preserve and protect holy relics'. He also thought that perhaps Templecombe preceptory was once used to house relics brought back from the Crusades, an idea that was echoed by George Tull in his book *Traces of The Templars*: 'It is not beyond the realms of possibility that the painting may have been imported into England via Bristol and thence brought to this remote preceptory in Somerset – who knows?'

We can only surmise as to the original meaning and purpose of this enigmatic image ...

Gazetteer

1086: There were two estates at Combe. One was held by Shaftesbury Abbey until the Dissolution, usually known as Abbas Combe, and a larger one was held by Odo, Bishop of Bayeux; this one was later to be granted to the Templars. Separate courts were recorded for each manor in the Middle Ages.[1]

The 1185 Templars' Inquest says that the Manor of Templecombe was given to the Knights Templar by Brother Serlo Fitz Odo, but that gift refers to the whole vill of Combe and as such may relate to West Combland in Buckland St Mary.[2] However, Combe may also have been granted to the Templars by the King;[3] or by William Martel, the King's Butler, before 1136.[4]

The 1396–7 Calendar of the Charters and Muniments of Templecombe contains a number of undated charters relating to the period before the suppression of the Templars:[5]

> no. 1: Charter of William Martel butler of the King of England of the Manor of Combe made to the Templars.
> no. 2: Quitclaim of Walter de Combe of all land with meadow and common in the close of Slademeade.
> no. 3: Quitclaim of John de Combe of common and pasture with on-coming and out-going of Berefurlong.
> no. 4: Release and quitclaim of Reynold the Templar of Worle, of 8 acres in the vill and fields of Templecombe.
> no. 5: Charter or quitclaim of Adam de Stawell of all rights and claims that he had in the Manor of Combe.
> no. 7: Concord between the brothers of the Temple of Combe and Thomas the Porter of pastures in open time [*tempore aperto*].
> no. 8: Concord between the brothers of the Temple of Combe and Julianna Abbess of Shaftesbury of common and pasture in Combe.

1185: Templecombe was listed as one of the appurtenances of Bristol. The vill of Combe was rented out to William de Combe, son of the priest, and W. Fitz Hugh at 13 marks per year for ten years.[6]

1206: The Pipe Rolls record that Adam Fitz Nigel owes 5 marks to/against the Master of the Knights Templars for land in Combe.[7]

1207–8: No. 6 in the 1396–7 Calendar is a Final Concord made in the Court of the King at Westminster in the ninth year of King John between Geoffrey Stawell (complainant) and Henry (then Custodian of Combe), (defendant) of the Manor of Combe.[8]

1240: The Bruton Cartulary says that Templars from Combe had been buried at Bruton Priory.[9]

1258: Nigel de Kingescot brought an action against Brother Amblard, Master of the Knights Templar of England for the Manor of Combe, but 'allowed the Master's right to it on receipt of 30 marks'.[10]

1260: The capital messuage of Temple Combe Manor is referred to in the Cal Patent Rolls 1258–66.[11]

1262–3: The Somerset Fines contains the following entry:

> At Ilchester, a final concord between Nigel de kingescot, claimant and Brother Amblard, Master of the Knights Templar in England, for the manor of Combe, except for a virgate of land in the same. Nigell acknowledged the manor, that is to say, whatever the Master held when the concord was made, to be the right of the Master and quit claimed to him. For this the Master gave Nigel thirty marks.[12]

(*See* entry for 1258.)

1308: In January all the Templars in England were arrested. These included three from Templecombe: William de Burton, Preceptor of Combe, John de Aley and Walter de Rokele, who were held in custody at Sherborne Castle.[13]

In October the first of the prisoners examined was William Raven who had been received into the Order at Templecombe before transferring to Cambridge.[14] The brothers from Templecombe were committed to the Tower.[15]

The 1396–7 Calendar (no. 12) was the Extent of the Manor of Templecombe taken by the Escheator of the King at the time of the Suppression of the Order of the Templars in England.[16] At the time the Templars had more than thirty cattle and their grange was stocked with wheat, maslin, peas, vetches, oats and malt.[17]

1312: On the suppression of the Templars, the estate passed to the Crown.[18] On 28 July an order was sent to the Keeper of the Templars' lands in Somerset stating that he was to pay to Alexander de Hunsingovere the following allowances, which the treasurer and barons of the exchequer had certified that he ought to receive for life:

> … his food for life at the brethren's table in the Templars' house at Combe; a suitable robe for a clerk or esquire at Christmas each year; a mark sterling each year, with the service of a groom; hay and oats for his horse as for one of the horses of the demesne stable of the preceptor of Combe; for so long as he [Alexander] labours about the affairs of the house.

When he was too old to work, the prebend of the oats was to be withdrawn, and he was only to receive hay for his horse (if he had one), and he was to give a moiety of his goods to the house at his death.[19]

1316–27+: Combe seems to have been held by Richard Lovel.[20]

1338–9: The Hospitaller Survey records the following for Templecombe:

> A capital messuage with a garden; 2 dovecotes; 368 acres of land; 60 acres of barren and exhausted land; 60½ acres of meadow; one small wood that was said to have been devastated by the occupiers after the suppression of the Templars, pasture for 33 oxen; separate pasture for 12 cows; pasture for 200 sheep; fixed rents of 23 marks 6s 7d.

The household was small, consisting only of three brothers and possibly ten servants. It needed to buy wheat, barley, malt and oats for baking and brewing. A chaplain, who received 20s per year, served the chapel at the preceptory. The estates of the preceptory were valued at £106 13s, including a small church at Bristol. Robert de Nafford, knight, was preceptor and there were two brethren under him besides a staff of seven servants.[21] Templecombe was the ninth wealthiest Hospitaller house in England.[22]

ENDNOTES

1. *SDNQ* Vol. li; The National Archives E318/19/993
2. Lees (1935), pp. 61–2; cxxxv; Knowles and Hadcock *Medieval Religious Houses* (Longman, London, 1974), p. 295; Dugdale Mon vi, p. 801. This is also the version given as no. 1 in the 1396–7 Calendar of the Charters and Muniments of Temple Combe *SDNQ* xxxi p. 86
3. Feudal Aids iv p. 289
4. This is the version given in the Inquest into the extent of Templar lands in Somerset and Dorset, NRA E142/111; Reg. Regum Anglo-Norm. iii p. xviii
5. *SDNQ* Vol. xxi, p. 86
6. Lees (1935), pp. 61–2
7. Pipe Rolls 8 John Mich 1206, p. 63
8. *SDNQ* Vol. xxi, p. 86
9. Bruton and Montacute Cartularies *Somerset Record Society* viii, p. 62
10. Victoria County History ii, p. 147; Somerset Feet of Fines *SRS* vi, pp. 202–3
11. Cal Patent Rolls 1258–66, p. 78
12. Somerset Fines *SRS* vol 6, pp. 202–3
13. TNA E142/111
14. Cal Patent Rolls 1313–17, p. 52
15. Wilkins Concilia ii, p. 347

16. *SDNQ* xxi p. 86
17. TNA E142/111
18. Victoria County History ii p. 147; Cal Mem Rolls 1326–7, pp. 347
19. Cal of the Close Rolls 1307–13, p. 468
20. Feudal Aids iv, p. 322; Cal Mem Rolls 1326–7, p. 347
21. Knights Hospitallers in England *Camden Society* (1857), pp. 183–6
22. *Archaeological Excavations at Templecombe, 1995* Somerset Archaeological and Natural History Society, p. 160

4

TEMPLE NEWBURY

In 1233–4, the Knights Templar were granted lands in Babington that are now part of Coleford, Hydon and other places. They were given by Robert de Gurnay who was acting on behalf of his grandfather, William de Harper (or Harptree), whose gift it was. It is possible that they may have held land here before that gift, probably a virgate in each of the manors of Luckington Walton and Kilmersdon.

In fact it appears that the Templars held much of the southern end of the parish of Babington below Newbury, an area of perhaps four virgates; one virgate in Luckington, one in Walton and a further virgate in Middlecote, which had formerly been part of Mells but had been incorporated into Babington by the Bishop of Coutances after the Conquest.

Historical background

The fact that the Templars held possessions near Coleford has been little noticed; the area has been associated more with coal mining than with the Knights Templars, though the matter was touched upon by Dr J.H. Harvey in respect of Hospitaller records at Winchester College which relate to Newbury Temple, during the period 1505–7.

The name Temple Newbury, or Newbury Temple, has now been forgotten, but it relates to the hamlet of Newbury, a short distance north of Coleford near Frome. During the time of its ownership by the Knights

Templar it was to become known as Temple Newbury, the name suggesting the Templars' 'new settlement'.

Other Templar holdings in the Coleford area included land at Holcombe, Kilmersdon, Luckington, Leigh on Mendip and Mells. These land grants were given mostly in the early 1200s. (*See* Gazetteer.)

Cloth making at Temple Newbury

Sheep were the animals that would have provided the largest revenue for the medieval farmer. Their skins were used for parchment, their milk could be made into cheese and, of course, their wool could be turned into cloth. It is highly likely that the fleeces from the Order's sheep at Temple Hydon on Mendip were processed at Temple Newbury. Woroth, probably near Middlecote, Mells, was also sheep-grazing land and this wool also would likely have been processed at Temple Newbury.

The process of turning wool to yarn for weaving consisted of several stages. Firstly it was 'carded'; this involved combing a small quantity of wool between wooden boards that were covered in small wires, or using the spiked plant teasel, which was deemed to be superior for the job. Carding produced a roll or ball that could then be spun into yarn.

Following carding, the wool was spun using a spinning wheel with treadle and flyer; this produced a yarn that could be woven into cloth on a wooden loom. During the early Middle Ages a vertical loom would have been used; in later years horizontal looms replaced these vertical looms.

All the preparation of the wool would have taken place in workers' cottages built close to the fulling mill. The remains of cottage 'platforms' have been found at Newbury that could possibly be of medieval origin, but whether these date from the Templar period, or indeed have any relationship to the mills, is not known.

In the 1185 Inquest it appears that the task of sheep washing and shearing, as well as spinning and weaving, frequently fell upon women. At Temple Rockley in Wiltshire this custom was very old, and had evidently been set down in pre-conquest tradition.

Once the cloth had been woven the next process was 'fulling'. A fulling mill cleans, shrinks and thickens or 'felts' the loosely woven fabric. Fullers' Earth is the cleansing material used for this process. Fuller's Earth was shipped into Bristol from the continent.

After cleansing, the fabric was beaten with two 'trip' hammers (stocks) projecting from the edge of a rotating wheel. This process, which was driven by water power, would have continued for long periods at a time, resulting in a heavily felted fabric that had shrunk considerably from its original size.

Once the fulling process was complete, the fabric would have been stretched on 'tentering frames', which resembled fences, and held in place with 'tenter hooks', until it was dry. The 'tentering frames' would have been placed in fields close to the mills.

It is believed that the Templars liked to oversee their own *'frères des metiers'* or lay brothers at their mills, rather than bringing in labour from outside their estates; this would suggest a strong Templar labour presence in the Temple Newbury area where, apart from the fulling mills, there was also a corn mill. This corn mill, situated at Coleford, is believed to be the oldest recorded corn mill in England.

The present-day mill was largely re-built in the 1700s, although some of the stone from the earlier building was probably reused. The present owner spoke of evidence of a tunnel running from the mill, under the field to the pub! This may have originally dated from the Templar period. There is also a very ancient bridge running over the river beside the mill, which leads to an old trackway doubtless used by the workers from the mill in early times.

The Corn Mill at Coleford. (Courtesy of Tristan Faith)

Above & below: *The old bridge near Coleford mill. (Courtesy of Tristan Faith)*

The river at Coleford provided water to power the Templar mills. (Courtesy of Tristan Faith)

Fulling mills

England became known for manufacturing a particularly good quality, heavy cloth that was highly sought after on the continent. This cloth was known as 'broadcloth' as it was 28–30 yards long and 5ft 3in wide and would have been made at the fulling mills in the Newbury area.

It is generally accepted that the Knights Templar introduced fulling mills to England from the East, as at the time of the Crusades fulling mills were in use throughout the Islamic world. Certainly, the first fulling mill recorded in England was in the 1185 Inquest of the Knights Templar; this was to be found at Temple Newsam. During the early medieval period the Templars were very much in the forefront of a minor Industrial Revolution that was happening in England and Europe.

The introduction of the 'mechanical' or water-powered fulling mill, as opposed to the earlier 'treading mills' (where cloth was trodden in urine by a 'fuller', 'tucker' or 'walker'), enabled the cloth to be manufactured more quickly and efficiently. The broadcloth produced at these mills was a much heavier higher quality product than its 'foot-fulled' counterpart, and was sought after both in England and Europe. It is believed that the wool and cloth produced in the South West of England largely contributed towards the wealth of the entire country from Domesday onwards.

Somerset appears to have been nationally important to the wool trade, and by the fourteenth and fifteenth centuries it was producing approximately a quarter of all England's wool, with Bristol being the main port for the export of cloth. During the Middle Ages the Temple and Redcliffe areas of Bristol were of great importance because of their textile and shipping industries. In 1299, use was granted of the Templar chapel (dedicated to St Katherine) to a Company of Weavers, St Katherine being the patron saint of weavers.

Coal workings

Evidence of surface coal workings were found near Page House that are believed may be of medieval origin, although whether they had anything to do with the Knights Templar or not is unknown. What is known, however, is that Bishop Reginald of Bath (1174) gave rights to mine lead and iron in Somerset at Hidun (high ground) on Mendip, and indeed anywhere in Somerset. Temple Hidun was land granted to the Templars at Hidun.

In 1235, a further charter, by Jocelin Bishop of Bath, gave licence for the mining of iron and for 'any other kind of mine' on Mendip. It doesn't take much of a leap of imagination to believe that the Templars were mining for coal at Temple Newbury and, as Coleford and Newbury became involved in coal mining in later centuries, it seems that the Templars usually exploited any natural resource readily available to them, and so the idea of them mining at Temple Newbury is very probable.

An unusual manor

It may be concluded then, that during the Templar period Temple Newbury held a position of considerable importance to the economic structure of Somerset, primarily due to its cloth industry.

In 1996, Dr John Harvey wrote a letter to Clive Wilkins commenting on Temple Newbury and its 'unusual manorial structure ... so different from the normal integrated manor'. It would seem that Templecombe had the same manorial structure; both of these manors consisted of widely separated lands and tenements. They included between them all the properties of the preceptory in Somerset except for Long Load.

At these two manors, courts were held for the mostly isolated holdings spread over a dozen or more parishes within a radius of 15–20 miles. Courts were generally held to resolve the minor disputes that so commonly occurred in the medieval countryside; these would often concern issues such as trespass by animals, theft of wood or other goods, disrepair of land or property and other such 'ordinary' happenings, as well as some offences of a more serious nature. They are all recorded in the English Court Rolls.

In form the courts, which included the View of Frankpledge, were held as if for a normal manor, although the practical difficulties of such a system must have been great.

There is some evidence that at one period separate courts were held at Temple Hydon, for tenants in the area of western Mendip between Worle and Harptree. By the end of the sixteenth century however, they all owed suit to Newbury in Babington or at Shepton Mallet where at least one court was held.

Page House

Evidence suggests that by 1279 Page House was the 'Capital Messuage' at the centre of the Templar estate, this was the 'free tenement' that Walter Page held from the Templars. In an assize of 1279 William Page (son) claims to have been unjustly 'disseised' of a messuage (probably Page

House), 2 acres of garden, 43 acres of land, 41 acres of wood and forest 6 acres of meadow and a rent of 5s and 6d. After the death of his father, he claims to have been 'disseised thereof' by Brother Roger le Mareschal, Brother William de C'estr and John Page. This was land and property that his father Walter Page had held by free tenure from the Templars.

As this dispute concerned Templar land and property, it was necessary for the Master of the Templars, Robert de Turville, to attend the court. Judgment was found in William's favour and he recovered his land and property. However, it was later found that Brother Robert and the others 'were not concerned in the disseisin, therefore they may go quit and William is in mercy. He was made to pay 10s damages for a false claim against them.[1] Page House Farm was built on or near the site of this tenement.

When the Templars first settled in England, the language they spoke would have been Norman French. This is sometimes echoed in place and field names in the lands that they acquired. The French influence is reflected in the Temple Newbury area, for example, fields near the Coleford sewage works are known as 'upper fryer moor', 'middle fryer moor' and 'lower fryer moor' ('fryer' is presumably synonymous with *frère* – ie brother's moor'). It appears these fields were adjacent to the fulling mill mentioned in the 1233–44 grant.

'La breche', meaning the breech, probably corresponds to an area on the west side of Page House Farm, and also formed part of the 1233–4 grant.

'La Lunemere', meaning the moon pool, is a large pond (now dry) near Page House. The 'old fish pond' mentioned in the grant is not La Lunemere, but is most likely the remains of the manorial fishponds, and would appear to be located near the stream known as 'Beversbroc'. It also seems likely that the main entrance to Page House was situated on the south side of the present house, not the north as it is today. This is indicated by an early road or track way on the south side, which would also appear to correspond to the 1233–44 grant.

Although the present farmhouse is largely seventeenth century, it does appear to have been constructed upon a much earlier ground plan. Whether this dates to the time of Templar occupation of the site is as yet unknown.

Gazetteer

The 1308 Inquest refers to Templar holdings in this area under the heading of 'Babington'.

Page House Farm. (Courtesy of Tristan Faith)

Templar lands at Page House. (Courtesy of Tristan Faith)

1228: The Fine Rolls of Henry III record that Walter Page gave 1 mark for having a writ to attaint the twelve jurors of an Assize of Mort D'Ancestor against Michael of Barton, concerning a tenement in Heydon.[2] Is this the same Walter Page who comes into prominence at Babington? Where was Heydon; possibly Mells or Radstock or elsewhere?

1233: The Fine Rolls of Henry III record that, on 20 June, Walter of Edmondsham gave the King 1 mark for having a writ that, 'the sheriff of Somerset is to cause the Assize of Novel Disseisin that the same Walter arraigned against Robert de Gournay and others concerning tenements in Babington and in Middlecott to come before R. of Lexington'.[3]

1233–4: Robert de Gurnay appointed William de Beverestan as attorney (*attornavit*) against an Emodesham tenant of 1 virgate and the fourth part of one virgate and 20 acres of land and two mills in Babinton.[4]

At Westminster in the octave of Trinity a Final Concord is recorded between Robert de Samford, Master of the Knights Templar in England (plaintiff) and Robert de Gurnay (defendant), of lands and mills in Harptree, Babington, Coleford and Middescot (Middlecote in Mells). These were to be given to the Master and Brethren of the Knights Templar as a gift from William the son of John, grandfather of Robert de Gurnay, whose heir he was, to hold of Robert and his heirs in 'frankalmoin' (free of all services and exactions). Robert warranted to the Master and Brethren of the Templars against all people and the Master received Robert into all the benefits and orisons in the House of the Knights Templar in England forever. Included in the grant in Babington and vicinity are the following:[5]

- 1¼ virgates with appurtenances formerly held by Wibert.
- An old fulling mill, which Henry Faber once held, with adjacent lands. (This probably corresponds with no. 84 in the 1396–7 Calendar, the grant by William, son of John de 'Harpentr', of one old fulling mill made to Walter de Emmondesham. It is incorrectly listed under charters for Worle.)
- All the land on the north of 'Beveresbroc', which was called 'la Breche'. (This was probably the 1¼ virgates held by Walter de Emodesham in 1233.[6] The toft called 'Orpytts', held by Thomas Orpyt of the Prioress of Buckland, referred to in the 1505 Rental was also probably part of the original area of 'la Breche'.)
- The corn mill in 'Culeford'.
- Another fulling mill, which Thomas de Walthon formerly held with all appurtenances, 'six acres … in the field eastward, and six acres in the

field westward'. (Both of the fulling mills seem to have been held by Walter de Emodesham in 1233–4.)[7]

- 1 virgate of land in 'Middescot', formerly held by Robert the Reeve. (Middlecote had once been part of Mells but became part of Babington after the Conquest. In the 1230s it would have been regarded as a tithing of Babington. This probably corresponds with Woroth in the 1505 Rental.[8] Harvey thought that in the 1505 Rental 'Woroth' must have been a large area of pasture high on Mendip, probably in Kilmersdon or Mells.)[9]
- All the land of Childeham of Beveresbroc as far as Lunemere.
- The tolls from the mill from the tenants of John in the parish of Babington. (This presumably refers to the corn mill in Coleford.)[10]

[The Master of the Knights Templar in England] The same puts in his place William de Dinelegh' against Robert de Gurnay on a plea of warrant of charter.[11]

1241: The Somerset Pleas contains the following entry; 'Robert de Gurnay against the Master of the Knights of the Temple in England on a plea of land by John son of Walter'. Another entry records that, 'Agnes, wife of Gervase de Hatton, against James de Chissedun on a plea of land, by Walter Page. On the next coming of the justices. He has pledged his faith. The same day is given in banco to Gervase, the husband of Agnes'. Is this the same Walter Page as earlier? If so, where was the land located?

It is also recorded that, 'Robert de Gurnay puts in his place John de Fernton against the Master of the Knights of the Temple in England on a plea of land etc'. Is this the same as the one above?[12]

1242–3: The Somersetshire Pleas contains the following entries:

Our lord the King notified the justices by his writ that Robert de Marisco had attorned before him in his place Jordan de Marisco to gain or to lose in a suit summoned before our lord the King by his writ of right between the aforesaid Robert, querent, and Walter le Page, tenant of one virgate and a quarter of land with the appurtenances in Bobinton, etc.[13]

Robert de Marisco seeks against Walter Page five ferlings of land with the appurtenances in Babinton, as his right, etc., and whereof Robert was seised as of fee and of right in the time of our lord the King that now is, taking there from profits to the value of 10s, etc. And Walter comes and vouches to warranty the Master of the Knights Templars in England. Let him have him on the octave of the Purification of the Blessed Mary by aid of the court. And Robert puts in his place Jordan de Marisco. [14]

(This suit seems to have ended in a fine levied at Westminster in the quinzaine of Easter.)

At Westminster in the quinzaine of Easter; between Robert de Marisco, claimant; and Walter Page, tenent; for a virgate of land and a quarter in Babinton. Robert quitclaimed to Walter; for this Walter gave Robert three marcs.[15]

William [note at bottom of the page Walter] Page gives half a mark for a licence to agree [*licencia concordandi*] to Robert de Marisco, on a plea of land, by the pledge of the same Robert. They have the chirograph [indented record of their final concord].[16]

1257: The Somersetshire Pleas records that:

The assize comes to recognise whether Osbert de Karevill, Walter le Page, and John le Blund, unjustly, etc, disseised Ralph de Karevill of his free tenement in Lokynton, since the first, etc, and whereon it is complained that they disseised him of one messuage and thirteen acres of land, with the appurtenances. Osbert and the others come, and say positively that they have not disseised Ralph of any free tenement, and thereon they put themselves upon the assize. The jurors say upon their oath that Osbert and the others have not disseised Ralph of any free tenement, because in truth Osbert at another time impleaded the said Ralph his brother in the court of our lord the King before his justices itinerant at Ivelcestr in the county of Somerset, so that by the consideration of the same court the said Osbert recovered his seisin against Ralph as well of the said messuage and thirteen acres of land, with the appurtenances, as of other land touching which he was impleaded. Whereof they say that the said Osbert and the others have not disseised him of any free tenement unjustly. Therefore it is considered that Osbert and the others [may go] quit thereof, and that Ralph de Carvill should take nothing by that assize, but should be in mercy for his false claim.[17]

Presumably this was where Luckington Farm is now, and within sight of Page House Farm; and this would be the same Walter Page.

1279: The Calendar of Patent Rolls contains the following:

Babington (Somers.) appointment of Walter de Wymburn and Thomas de S. Vigor to take the Assise of Novel Disseisin arraigned by William Page against Roger le Mareschal and others, touching a tenement in; and the similar assise arraigned by the same demandant against John Page, touching a tenement in Mells.

Babington (Somers.) appointment of Walter de Wimborne and Thomas de S. Vigor to take the assize of mort d'ancestor arraigned by John Page of Babington against William Page, touching possessions in.[18]

An assizes at Montacute, 16 August 1279:

The assize comes to recognise whether Brother Roger le Mareschal, Brother William de Cestr and John Page unjustly etc. disseised William Page of his free tenement in Babinton after the first etc. whereof he complains that they disseised him of a messuage, 43 acres of land, 6 acres of meadow, 40 acres of waste and a rent of five shillings and six pence in the same town.

And John Page, who is the tenant, comes and he answers for himself and for all the others and he says that that tenement was of one William Page who died seised thereof and who held the tenement of the master of the Knights Templars in England, and the master, immediately after the death of William, seised the tenement into his hand and afterwards enfeoffed this John Page and because the master is not named in the writ he asks for judgement whether the assize in this case ought to proceed.

And William Page cannot deny this, therefore it is considered that Roger and the others may go without a day and William is in mercy for a false claim.[19]

The Somersetshire Pleas also lists an Attain of Jury taken before Walter de Wymburn and Thomas de Sancto Vigore at Briwton 10 September 1279:

The assize comes to recognize whether Brother Robert de Tureuill, Master of the Knights Templars in England, Brother Roger le Mareschal, Brother William de Cestr and John Page unjustly etc. disseised William Page of his free tenement in Babinton after the first etc. whereof he complains that they disseised him of a messuage and two acres of garden and 43 acres of land, 41 acres of wood and forest and six acres of meadow and a rent of five shillings and sixpence in the same town.

And Brother Robert and all the others excepting John Page come, and they say they have nothing and claim nothing in those tenements, and that they did not disseise William of the tenements, they put themselves on the assize.

And John Page who holds the tenements comes, and he says that those tenements were of one Walter his father and that he died seized thereof and immediately after Walter's death he himself entered the tenements as his son and heir and that this is so he puts himself on the assize.

The jury say that John disseised William of the tenements which he put to their view, unjustly etc. Therefore it is considered that William shall recover his seisin of those tenements by view of the recognitors and John is in mercy. And they say that Brother Robert and the others were not concerned in the disseisin, therefore they may go quit and William is in mercy for a false claim against them.

Damages 10s all [paid] to the clerk.[20]

1280: John Page brought a Writ of Entry about a mill in Babinton against Roger Coleford and then asked for licence to withdraw from his writ, and he has it.[21]

Two other Writs of Entry for this year concerned 'Henry, Abbot of Kyngeswode'.

Henry abbot of Kyngeswode seeks against Robert Page a mill in Babyntone which he claims to be the right of his church of Kyngeswode and in which Robert has entry by Walter Page who unjustly etc. disseised Thomas once abbot of Kyngeswode, a predecessor of the aforesaid abbot, after the first etc.

And Robert comes: and denies his right when etc. and he says that he ought not to answer him on this writ because he says that he does not hold the mill and that he did not hold it on the day he took out his writ.

And abbot Henry cannot deny this.

Therefore it is considered that Robert may go without a day thereon and the abbot is in mercy.[22]

Henry abbot of kingeswode seeks against John le Jouene 16 acres of land in Bakynton which he claims to be the right of his church of kingeswode and in which John has entry only by Robert Page to whom Walter Page demised them who unjustly etc. disseised Thomas late abbot of kingeswode a predecessor of the aforesaid prior after the first etc.

And John comes: and on another occasion he vouched to warranty thereon Robert Page who came by summons and warranted him and he [Robert] vouched lastly to warranty thereon John Page who now comes by summons; and he warrants him and he denies the right of the abbot when etc. and he freely acknowledges that Walter Page his father demised that land to Robert Page but he says that Walter did not unjustly etc. disseise Thomas late abbot etc. because Walter entered the tenements by feoffment of the master of the

Knights Templar in England who feoffed Walter therein by his charter which he made to him thereon: and that this is so he asks for an enquiry: and the abbot likewise, there fore let a jury be made thereon.

The jury say that Walter entered the tenements by feoffment of the master of the Knights Templar in England and not by disseisin.

Therefore it is considered that Walter entered the tenements by feoffment of the master of the Knights Templar in England and not by disseisin.

Therefore it is considered that John may go without a day thereon and that the abbot shall take nothing by that writ but he is in mercy for a false claim.

In margin. Thursday after three weeks from S. John (16 July).[23]

Another assize concerned 'William Fraunceys of Middelcote':

The assize comes to recognise whether William Fraunceys of Middelcote unjustly etc. disseised John Page of his free tenement in Melles within the summons of the eyre etc. whereon he complains that he disseised him of one acre of land and a place which contains 10 feet in length and 24 perches in width etc.

And William, by Geoffrey his bailiff, comes: and he says that the land is not in Melles but in Middelcote: and if it should be found that the land is in Melles he says that he did no injury or disseisin for he says that John Page never was in seisin of that land as of free tenement so that he could be disseised of it and on this he puts himself on the assize: and John likewise, therefore let the assize be taken.

The jury say that John never was in seisin of the said tenements as of free tenement so that he could be disseised thereof.

Therefore it is considered that William may go without a day thereon and that John shall take nothing by that assize but he is in mercy for a false claim etc.[24]

1296–7: The Somersetshire Pleas record:

At Westminster in the octave of the Purification; between John son of Geoffrey Dyme, querent; and John Page and Nichola his wife, impediments; for a messuage, a carucate of land, ten acres of meadow, forty acres of wood, two hundred acres of Heath, and thirty shillings rent, in Babyngton, Mellis, Leydon, Middelcote, Worthe, Lokyngton and Walton. Plea of warranty of deed was summoned. John and Nichola acknowledge the right of John Dyme as by their gift; for this John Dyme granted the same to John Page and Nichola, to hold to them and the heirs of their bodies, of him, rendering yearly one rose at Midsummer and doing to the chief lords of the fee for him all other services; and he warranted the same. If it happen that John Page shall die without heirs of his body, then after the decease of both John and Nichola, the said tenement shall wholly revert to John Dyme, to hold of the chief lords of the fee by the services belonging.

(Endorsed.) Henry de Wiltes Brother of John de Wiltes put in his claim.[25]

Compare the entry below for 1315–16 'a messuage, a carucate of land and ten acres of meadow in Babington, Lokynton, Walton, Middlecote and Melles'; were any of these former Templar possessions?

1304–5:

Eodem modo mon R. Geoffrey Samuel of Melles that he himself in the Court of the King at Taunton recovered his seisin against John Page of Babyngton and others for fifty shillings rent with appurtenances in Babyngton & Kynerersdon, etc.[26]

1314–15: The hamlet of Middelcote together with the manor and the advowson chapel were recorded as being held by the heirs of John ap Adam for 2½ knights' fees.[27] Does this refer to the Templars' part of Middlecote?

ENDNOTES

1. Somersetshire Pleas *SRS* vol. xli, pp. 228–9
2. Fine Rolls Henry III Vol. 12, p. 183
3. ibid Vol. 17, p. 232
4. Close Rolls 18 Henry III, p. 544
5. ibid
6. ibid
7. ibid
8. Harvey, 'Templar Holdings in East Somerset' *SDNQ* Vol. xxxi p. 141
9. ibid, p. 137
10. Somerset Fines *SRS* Vol. vi, pp. 77–8
11. Curia Regis Rolls 17–18 Henry III Vol. 15, p. 163
12. Somersetshire Pleas SRS Vol. xi, p. 129
13. ibid Vol. xi, pp. 144–5
14. ibid Vol. xi, p. 163
15. ibid Vol. vi, p. 112
16. Curia Regis Rolls 26–7 Henry III Vol. xvii, p. 370
17. Somersetshire Pleas *SRS* Vol. xi, p. 404

18. Appendix to the forty-eight report of the Deputy Keeper of the Public Records: No 1 Calendar of Patent Rolls: 7 Edward I 1887, p. 10
19. Somersetshire Pleas *SRS* Vol. xli, p. 216
20. ibid Vol. xli, pp. 228–9
21. ibid Vol. xliv, p. 51
22. ibid, pp. 137–8
23. ibid, pp. 152–3
24. ibid, p. 337
25. Somerset Fines *SRS* Vol. vi, p. 301
26. *Rotulorum Originalium in Curia Scaccarii Abbreviato Temporibus Regum Hen. III Ed.I & Ed. II*, Vol. 1 (1805)
27. Inquisitions Post Mortem Edward II Vol. 5 *Her Majesty's Stationary Office* (1908), p. 339

5

CAMELEY AND TEMPLE CLOUD

Resign thy kingdom to me, for I bear the Mark of royalty on my shoulder
(Jordan de Marisco's henchman, the 'would be' assassin of Henry III)

Cameley is a small and beautiful village, seemingly lost in time, nestling close to the Cam Brook near the Chew Valley in Somerset. It is situated just off the A37, and the ancient parish of Cameley incorporates other villages, including Temple Cloud. Cameley is approximately 10 miles from both Bristol and Bath.

During the Middle Ages there were two separate 'vills' or country estates within the parish of Cameley: Cameley itself and Cloud (there are various spellings for 'Cloud').

During the twelfth century the de Alnes (or d'Alneto) family held Cameley and in about 1150 they gave the manor to the priory of St Peter in Bath. However, it would appear that the de Mariscos were holding Cameley by the start of the thirteenth century when 'all the vill of Cameley' passed into the hands of the Templars. There are field names that remain on the 1760 Hippisley estate map reminding us of the Templars' legacy at Cameley; these are Outer Temple Field, Inner Temple Field, and Temple Mead. As yet, there is no information as to exactly when the Templars acquired Cloud.

How the Templars came to acquire Cameley and Temple Cloud is intimately bound up with not only the story of the de Mariscos and their illegal possession of Lundy Island, but also, as our research has led us to discover, the involvement of a hitherto overlooked but exceedingly important baronial family, the St Maurs.

Temple Field, showing strip lychetts. (Courtesy of Alex Meadows)

The history of the Templars acquisition and loss of Cameley and Temple Cloud can only be glimpsed through the mists of time, and many questions remain unresolved, therefore the entire story is still rather a mystery!

Historical background 1066–1202

In 1066, two thanes, Sheerwald and Ordwald, held Cameley in two almost equal proportions. It appears likely that these two manors were what later became the manors of Cameley and Temple Cloud.

By 1086, the Bishop of Coutances held the parish of Cameley and it is said 'Humphrey held one hide of this manors land, in lordship'.

From 1135, during King Stephen's reign, the de Mariscos are mentioned for the first time in connection with the Isle of Lundy.

In 1140/53, Alexander de Alneto, his brothers and their mother gave the manor of Cameley and seventy silver marks to the monks of St Peter's Priory (now the Abbey), Bath. This gift was confirmed by William, Earl of Gloucester and Henry, Duke of Normandy. Along with the manor, the monks presumably acquired the church at Cameley, which is recorded as in their hands by the late 1100s.

In 1155, Henry II demanded the return of all the lands that had been granted away during King Stephen's reign. He was particularly anxious to prevent attack from the French, and was keen to take possession of the English Islands; this included the Isle of Lundy, which he then granted to the Templars. The de Mariscos refused to comply with the King's request, and remained in possession of the island, and from that time onwards caused all manner of problems for the English kings.

Cameley was the dower of William de Marisco's wife, Lucie de Alneto, who is buried with their son Jordan and Grandson William in Bath Abbey. However, between 1175 and 1188 the d'Alnetos took back the Manor of Cameley that had previously been granted to Bath Priory, and granted the monks the church of Long Ashton instead!

In July 1189, King Richard the Lionheart confirmed the grant of Lundy to the Templars. However, William de Marisco still refused to hand it over to them, for which he was fined 200 marks and outlawed. By 1197, however, he was back in favour and to be found fighting for the King in France.

By 1200, King John confirmed that the island belonged to the Templars, but they had to pay £1,000 for this privilege. William pledged his manor at Huntspill to guarantee his gift of Lundy to the Templars, but the island was still not handed over. By this time, William and his supporters were plying a trade in piracy from Lundy and, strangely enough, neither the King nor the Templars seemed able or willing to do anything about this situation!

In 1201–2, confirmation is found of a grant to the Templars of 'all the land of William de Marisco in Huntspill and Cameley'. King John confirmed this grant, but still the de Mariscos remained in possession.

The de Mariscos – The Pirates of Lundy

William de Marisco was one of Henry I's illegitimate children. The de Marisco family, whose coat of arms bore a lion rampant, the lion of England, therefore believed (perhaps justifiably) that they had a valid claim to the English throne. The de Mariscos were to prove a troublesome and lawless lot and a thorn in the side of several English kings. They held the Island of Lundy for about 200 years.

That being said, there were other members of the family who were not so rebellious and indeed were highly regarded, such as the priest and Oxford Franciscan scholar Adam de Marisco, who was known throughout Europe as Dr Illustris, and was a friend of Roger Bacon; also Richard de Marisco, who was Lord Chancellor and Bishop of Durham. However, it was the branch of the family connected with Cameley, Huntspill, Temple Cloud and Lundy Island that are of interest to our story, and they came to be known as the Pirates of Lundy.

By 1202, during the reign of King John, Lundy Island was cut off from essential supplies, because the Sheriff of Devon was forced to defend his ports against William de Marisco, who was by now regularly using Lundy as a base to attack ships and traders along the North Devon coast. Strangely enough, in 1204 the King granted William the Manor of Braunton, and appointed him as head of some of his galleys! Perhaps this was a 'sweetener' to try and encourage loyalty not rebellion; this was clearly unsuccessful because by 1217, William had sided with many of the English barons in supporting Louis of France against King John at the Battle of Sandwich. Some of the shipping for this attack was provided by Eustace the Monk, another pirate, who was described by Powicke in his book *The Thirteenth Century*, as 'the most famous sailor-adventurer of his time ... whose exploits became legendary'. Eustace was captured and beheaded after the battle.

William was amongst the prisoners taken alongside Louis' men, and he was put in prison for his part in the battle. Whilst William was at sea, the King seized Lundy, and William's wife, four sons and two daughters were captured.

The following year, by which time Henry III had acceded to the throne, peace was negotiated and all prisoners that had been captured and imprisoned after the battle, including William, were released.

Surprisingly, William was given back his island, and, still more surprisingly, the King must have believed him trustworthy, as he allowed him to remove his mangonels (stone throwers) from his lands at Cameley to Lundy! He did however incur a fine of £11 4s for previously retaining possession of the island.

In 1220, the Templars were given 100s in recompense for the loss of Lundy. This is confirmed by a charter dated 1227 in which Henry III re-affirmed the grants of his father to the Templars. Lundy was omitted from this charter, indicating its return to the de Mariscos.

Just three years later, in 1225, William de Marisco died peacefully in his bed, and was succeeded by his son Jordan.

Unfortunately, the trouble was not over for Henry III. The late William had a brother, Geoffrey, who was Justiciar of Ireland, and Geoffrey had a son who was also named William, neither of these de Mariscos appeared to have caused any serious problem until Geoffrey's 'friend' Richard Marshall's rebellion against the King. The term 'friend' is used very loosely, because there is some doubt as to Geoffrey de Marisco's friendly intentions here; some even suggest he was responsible for Richard's death, but that is another story! Richard Marshall was injured during the rebellion and eventually died (or was murdered) at Kilkenney Castle.

Geoffrey de Marisco had apparently tried to remain loyal to the King during the uprising, but following its failure, and Richard's death, Geoffrey and his son William, plus three of their relatives, were imprisoned by Henry III. Even after their release King Henry was clearly suspicious of them and seized three of their castles in Ireland as a warning.

Soon afterwards, a new Justiciar of Ireland was appointed, which caused both Geoffrey and William to travel to London in an attempt to show their loyalty to the King and clear their names. Shortly after their arrival however, the King's envoy, Henry Clement, who had already had detrimental exchanges with the de Mariscos concerning the rebellion in Ireland, was killed, and William was suspected of his murder.

William, unsurprisingly, fled to Lundy with his supporters and family, whilst Geoffrey and others sought sanctuary at the Hospital of St John at Clerkenwell. The King immediately outlawed William, and the others implicated in Henry Clement's death, and his lands in Ireland were confiscated. Geoffrey and his men were, however, allowed their freedom.

Upon arrival on Lundy Island William was met by his cousin, another William, who was Jordan de Marisco's son and therefore rightful occupier of the island. William, son of Jordan, did not want any dealings with this outlaw relative, and wrote to the King asking for safe passage to England, and the right to 'retire there'. This was granted.

Once established on the Island, William followed in his uncle's footsteps and turned to a life of piracy; it wasn't long before his thoughts turned again to treason.

On 8 September 1238, whilst Henry was holding court at Woodstock, a man who claimed he was sent by William de Marisco confronted him with the words 'resign thy kingdom to me, for I bear the mark of royalty on my shoulder'. The King was unperturbed, believing it to be the ravings of a mad man. That very night, however, the same man entered the King's chamber armed with a knife with the intention of murdering him. Fortunately, the King was not in the chamber at the time, and the man was seized by the guard, confessed to his murderous intentions, and was tried and executed.

From that point onwards the King made a concerted effort to capture William and his fellow rogues, and on 2 January 1242, a party led by the Norfolk baron William Bardolf set out to Lundy Island to capture William de Marisco and his fellow rogues.

It is said that one of William's own men betrayed him, and assisted the baron and his men in William's capture, with their knowledge of the island.

The outlaws were taken first to Bristol and then to the Tower of London, where they were all sentenced to death. It was there, on 25 July 1242, that William de Marisco was hung, drawn and quartered, and his four quarters sent to the four principal cities of England. Some say he was the first traitor to meet his death in such a manner.

Was this the end of the de Marisco story? Well, unsurprisingly, it was not, because the 1284–5 Feudal Aids record that 'John de Marisco holds the vill of Cameley by the service of one knight's fee', and in 1303 that 'Herbert de Marisco held Cameley by the service of one knight's fee'. Clearly the de Mariscos had returned to reclaim the land that they believed was rightfully theirs, although they never again reclaimed Lundy.

The de Sancto Mauros (St Maur)

The St Maurs were an ancient and noble Norman family, who were of baronial stock before they came to England at the Conquest. Wido de St Maur is recorded in the somewhat unreliable Battle Abbey Rolls, and from 1066 to 1090 his son William Fitz-Wido held a barony in Somerset, Wiltshire and Gloucestershire and ten manors in Somerset, including Portishead. The family also held Penhow Castle not far from Cardiff. The church at Penhow is dedicated to the Abbot of St Maur, the small monastic village in France from where the Sancto Mauros originated. Researcher Joe Silmon Monerri has concluded that this is St Maur des Bois, in the Avranches region of Normandy. The coat of arms of the St Maurs in the early days was simply Argent, two Chevrons Gules – that is a white or silver background, with two red chevrons.

It has been extremely difficult to try and put together a precise genealogy of the St Maurs, as there are so many conflicting sources and to add to the melee, certain members of the Seymour family, the 'Dukes of Somerset', have attempted to link themselves with the illustrious name of St Maur! The history of the Somerset St Maurs and how they relate to the story of the Knights Templar in Somerset is complicated. One thing which is certain is that the St Maurs have no connection with the Seymours, and that the branch of the St Maur family with which this book is concerned came to an end with Richard St Maur, Lord of Castle Cary, in about 1400 when he died without male issue and no male heir.

The Cameley connection

The depiction of the Royal Arms of England (three lions) on the north post of the chancel arch in the church at Cameley is suggestive of a high level of patronage which would seem unusual in a small church in deepest Somerset. It is rare to find the royal arms depicted in a church prior to when Henry VIII became head of the Church of England in 1534.

On the south post of the chancel arch there is another coat of arms with two red chevrons. It has previously been recorded that these arms represent the de Clares, Earls of Gloucester, whose arms were: Or, (gold or yellow), three chevrons gules (red). However, it is apparent that there had been a mistake in the identification of this coat of arms, as they are clearly not the arms of the de Clares but the Argent (silver or white), two chevrons gules (red) of the St Maur family. The identification was confirmed by Dr Clare Ryder, archivist at Temple Church, London, who supplied a photograph of a stained glass window of Almeric St Maur showing his shield with coat of arms.

There is a documented connection of the family of St Maur with (Temple) Cloud and also there was a connection of the parish of Cameley with the Knights Templars from the beginning of the thirteenth century. At this time the Master of the Templars in England was Almeric St Maur. It is highly likely therefore that the coat of arms in the church was that of Almeric St Maur and that the church was, therefore, connected with the Templars. Alternatively, were they the arms of another more local member of the family, Ralph of St Maur Lord of (Temple) Cloud, in the same parish?

If the arms do indeed belong to Almeric St Maur, it is a fair assumption that, as the Templars became lords of the vill of Cameley in 1201–2 and it is accepted that both arms were painted during the same period, the Royal Arms portrayed on the chancel arch are most likely those of King John, 1199–1226. There is also suggestion that the owners of these two coats of arms were of such importance that they were seen as guardians of the gateway to the altar and sanctuary of the church.

Almeric de St Maur

Almeric (spelt variously as Americ, Emmeri, Aimery and Aymeric) was Master of the Knights Templar in England from 1200–18. He was an exceedingly important figure, and frequently served as advisor to King John, who relied heavily on the Templars for support during his reign.

Almeric's life-long and closest friend is said to have been William Marshall, Earl of Pembroke. William Marshall often fought alongside the Templars in the Holy Land and, as will be shown later, was received into the Order just before his death in 1219.

King John depended on the advice and co-operation of the Templars in many of his affairs of state, and frequently fled to New Temple in London for refuge when the going became tough! New Temple was the

The three lions of England. (Courtesy of Alex Meadows)

The St Maur coat of arms. (Courtesy of Alex Meadows)

place where most of the Royal Treasury was deposited, and John was staying there when the barons made their demands, which culminated in the creation of the Magna Carta. It was Almeric who advised him in the creation of the charter, and was with him on the momentous occasion of its signing at Runnymede. Almeric is in fact mentioned in the first paragraph of the charter; his name is amongst those of the most important dignitaries.

In 1202, there was a grant and concord between Nicol de Kivilly (claimant) and Henneri St Maur, Master, (tenant) concerning the lands of William de Marisco in Cameley. 'Henneri' must be a mis-reading for Almeric (pronounced Emery) as he was Magister or Master of the Templars at this time.

In 1203, Almeric witnessed the charter that agreed the dowry of King John's wife Isabella of Angouleme, and in 1204, Almeric was sent as the King's envoy to Normandy. Whilst he was Provincial Master, King John had many financial dealings with the Temple.

In 1215, Almeric lent him 1,100 marks to obtain troops from Poitou, and when John made his submission to the Pope at Temple Ewell, Almeric gave him a gold mark for the offering.

Some sources say that Almeric died abroad, but there is a very early source, 'L'Histoire de Guillaume Marechal' that tells a different story. 'L'Histoire' is a French chronicle written soon after William Marshall's death at the request of his family; this was commonplace amongst the nobility during the Middle Ages, as it provided a record, or keepsake of the departed. It is therefore accepted that 'L'Histoire de Guillaume Marechal' is a true record of events. It is this document that tells us of the final days of Almeric St Maur.

It was mentioned earlier that William Marshall, who was known as the greatest knight in Christendom, was a close friend of Almeric Master of the Temple. 'L'Histoire' recounts that when William lay dying, he summoned his old and trusty friend to his side, so that he may be received into the Order. A Templar mantle had been made for this purpose some years previously. Almeric himself was not a well man, but he travelled to be at his friend's side at the earl's manor at Caversham. It is said that it was long ago, in the Holy Land, that William had told Almeric of his wish to be received into the Order before death, and thus it was that Almeric started to make preparations for William's reception.

Tragically, on his return to London, Almeric's own illness overtook him, and he died. 'L'Histoire' tells us that Almeric had requested that his body be buried before the High Altar, in the round of Temple Church, that he may 'rest by the side of Brother William the Marshall, whose fellowship he had loved in this world and hoped also to enjoy in heaven'. William Marshall himself died a few days later, and both were buried side by side before the High Altar in the round of Temple Church, London.

As yet, it remains a mystery where in the St Maur family tree Almeric fits, only that he had the same coat of arms as other members of the St Maur family, and that another member of the St Maur family had land at Temple Cloud during the same period; this was Ralph of St Maur.

Ralph of St Maur

The Curia Regis Rolls document that Ralph of St Maur was the son of Thomas St Maur and his wife Juliane. He had an older brother, Peter, and another brother, Milo. Thomas and Juliane also had a daughter named Rohesia.

Ralph's maternal grandfather was Anketil, though whether this was the frequently documented 'Anketil of Chewton' is unknown, as Anketil was a common name at the time.

In 1204, there was a dispute between Ralph of St Maur and William de Marisco and de Marisco brought a Writ of Novel Disseisin against Ralph of St Maur concerning land at Cloud in the parish of Cameley. The following year Ralph brought a similar action against William de Marisco.

Jury knobbling!

In the 1204–5 dispute it would appear that the jury of twelve who swore that Ralph of St Maur had never had seisin of his land, had been bribed by William de Marisco (a serious offence, even in the thirteenth-century). In 1205, a new jury of twenty-four was called, and they found against the twelve who 'swore falsely' that Ralph had never had seisin of his land. William de Marisco was fined 20*s*.

Ralph claimed that he had been 'given the charters by Anketil on his death bed', and then he had gone before the hundred court of Chewton. After this he went to Cloud, broke the door of the dovecotes, took doves, and then went into the garden and took apples. This would have been his way of showing he was lord of the manor, of affirming his rights!

Ralph's manor was East Court, Temple Cloud. In 1568–9, the manor is recorded as consisting of:

Manor house
Barn
Stall
Malt house
Bake house
Garden
Orchard
Barton
Dovecote

In Ralph's time it is likely to have consisted of similar elements, probably with the inclusion of fishponds, which were usual in a manorial complex.

It has also been found that the old track way named Temple Way, or Temple Lane End, follows the parish boundary from Cholwell to Cameley and ends at East Court.

Other members of the St Maur family in Somerset

Geoffrey St Maur: At the time of the 1185 Inquest, Geoffrey (also spelt Galfridus, Geoffroi) St Maur was Lord of Clayhanger in Devon and Williton in Somerset. Williton was a gift to the Templars by Reginald Fitz Urse, who had inherited the estate from his father in 1168. The Templars acquired it in 1171, which is presumably close to the time when Geoffrey became tenant. Fitz Urse was one of the murderers of Thomas Becket and he gave his land at Williton to the Templars to atone for the death of the archbishop, and also went on crusade. Fitz Urse probably died in the Holy Land, though some believe he survived the Crusades and went to Ireland.

Lawrence St Maur: Lawrence (Laurence) St Maur held Rode in Somerset in 1274. Records state that he was granted the right to hold a market there on Thursday of each week, and a fair every year on the feast day of St Margaret. He married Sibilla and had one son, Nicholas.

In 1282, he acknowledged the service of half a knight's fee for his inheritance in Wiltshire and one third of a knight's fee for Sibilla's inheritance in Northumberland.

In 1295, he was exempted from general summons of persons holding land by military tenure for the King's expedition to Gascony. It is believed he was a crusader at the time of Edmund Crouchback.

Nicholas St Maur: Nicholas was the son of Lawrence, he was born at Rode (date unknown) and died in 1316 at Kingston Seymour. His first wife was Eva de Meysey and his second wife was Helen (she survived him). He had one son, Thomas. Nicholas performed military service against the Scots on numerous occasions. He was summoned to Parliament in 1314 as Baron St Maur.

Peter St Maur: The 1185 Inquest tells us that Peter St Maur was Lord of Portishead and Weston (in Gordano). He gave Portishead to the Templars. This was probably the same Peter who was the elder brother of Ralph and Milo.

Milo St Maur: Milo was Lord of Kingston Seymour (formerly Kingston St Maur). He was also one of the rebel Barons at the time of the Magna

Carta. He is mentioned in a Fine Roll for the period along with his first wife Agnes. His second wife was Cecily. Milo was born at the family seat of Penhow, and it is believed he had two sons.

The Inquest also mentions a Simon St Maur, who was a member of the Templar Order at that period, but as yet there is no further information about him.

The end of the family line

There were many other members of the St Maur family who held extensive lands in other counties across England. In Somerset, a piece of medieval stained glass bearing the St Maur arms was discovered in a window at Blackford Church, near Castle Cary; this manor was held by Nicholas St Maur in 1362. Also found was evidence about their holding the Manor of Bratton St Maur (or Seymour), near Carey. Bratton was also held by Nicholas St Maur. He acquired this estate in 1351 through his marriage to Muriel Lovel, a child bride. Muriel bore him two sons, Nicholas and Richard. She died when the boys were aged just six and three. Nicholas died in 1361, followed not long afterwards by his elder son. This left the younger son, Richard, then only nine years old, as heir to his father's estates in Somerset, which included Castle Cary, Southbarrow, Northbarrow, Bratton, Marsh (their chief place of residence) and the borough of Wincanton. As Richard was a minor, he was ward of King Edward III.

Richard St Maur was the last of the male line of the Somerset St Maurs; his death in 1400 left an only daughter, Alice, who married Sir William Zouche. And so it was that the lands in Somerset belonging to the noble and illustrious family of St Maur passed from their hands …

Richard Engayne

The Engayne family were a notable family from Normandy that were given lands in Buckinghamshire at the Conquest. Richard Engayne was a Templar, and appears to have had connections with Somerset, although it is not known which preceptory he belonged to; presumably it would have been either Bristol or Templecombe.

In 1310, one of the thirty-one captive Templars questioned at the Tower of London was Brother Thomas Wothrope. Brother Thomas said he had known Richard Engayne personally. During the trial Richard is referred to as a 'Templar fugitive', implying that he either escaped or avoided capture.

By 1315, after the dissolution of the Templars, Richard must have been (re) captured, because he appears in Bishop John Drokensford's register. Drokensford was Bishop of Bath and Wells. Richard appears on the register as one of the Templars assigned to do penance at Taunton Priory, at the cost of 4*d* a day.

The mystery deepens when, in 1327, his name turns up in the Lay Subsidy Returns for Temple Cloud! Could it be that he served his penance and was then released, or did he merely leave the priory after matters concerning the Templars had gone quiet? He may have had family at Temple Cloud; we may never know for sure.

Cameley Church

'I know few churches where building, churchyard and surrounding fields and stream are more in harmony,' says Simon Jenkins in his book *England's Thousand Best Churches*. He then goes on to speak of the church tower, and suggests that it 'seems to have been sent from afar to protect a local secret'.

The exterior of Cameley Church. (Courtesy of Simon Brighton)

The interior of Cameley Church, looking west. (Courtesy of Simon Brighton)

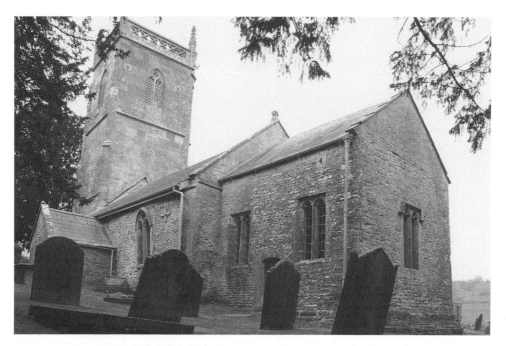

Cameley Church, showing original small Romanesque church, and tower added at a later date. (Courtesy of Alex Meadows)

This is certainly how it is with Cameley; on the one hand the visitor experiences a peaceful pastoral scene, on the other, a strange air of quiet expectation pervades, as if something were about to happen, or some ancient mystery about to be revealed ...

Cameley Church was originally built in Romanesque style. It is twelfth century in origin, but has many later additions and changes. It is dedicated to St James of Compostela. Dedications to this saint were rare before the twelfth century, during which time there was an awakened interest in pilgrimages to the saint's shrine at Compostela. St James was one of the Templars' favoured saints, and this is one of the pilgrim routes that they protected.

The chancel arch and nave date from around 1200. The tower that is built in red sandstone, and rather out of keeping with the rest of the tiny church, is fifteenth century.

The church contains a number of wall paintings that range in date from the twelfth-century 'Templar' period to the fifteenth century. There is a fine, but rather strange jester or 'knave' on the north wall behind the pulpit, thought to date from 1300. He is strange because he has a hare-lip and forked tongue and appears to be holding a scroll of some sort!

The jester or knave. (Courtesy of Simon Brighton)

Also on the north wall, above the hat pegs, are some very early designs that show a geometric, floriate design with petals. This design has been found at other locations connected with the Templars, who had an expert knowledge of geometry and symbolism. The number eight, amongst other things, is the number of eternity; it is a highly significant number in the Bible, and occurs many times at Templar sites. However, the wall paintings that are of particular importance to this book are the previously mentioned coats of arms on the chancel arch.

It is interesting that there are no recorded incumbents at the church during the period of Templar occupation. This could bear out the theory that the Templars put their own clergy in the churches of the manors that they held. The first recorded incumbent at Cameley is in 1297.

Two wooden carvings

In around 1200, there was a probable rebuilding of the church. According to John Blair, the nave, south door, external eastern quoins, the altar recess and probably the chancel arch, were all of good quality work, suggestive of a single phase of building.[1] Blair however, makes no comment on the Royal Coat of Arms painted on the chancel arch, nor would he seem to know of the Templars' connection with Cameley about this time.

During repair work on the late medieval roof of the church in 1959, a discovery was made of a small Romanesque beakhead, carved in oak and of owl-like appearance. The beakhead is a very rare survivor of a style of wooden carving that Blair believes would suggest 'top-level patronage' in a minor country church. He suggests that the link with the monks from the priory at Bath accounts for this high-level work. However, evidence strongly suggests that it was King John and the Templars who were in fact the 'top-level 'patrons of Cameley church.

At the same time that the beakhead was discovered, a carved wooden man's head was also found. The man's head has caused a great deal of controversy, which will be discussed at greater length in the closing chapter of the book. The man's head is life-sized, and depicts a man with long hair, an open mouth, prominent nose, and small, forked beard. He is surrounded by a criss-cross or 'trellis' border. Thus far, the type of wood the image is carved from, and the actual date of the artefact remain unknown, although clearly it is very old. Upon seeing the head, Dr Michael Costen, formerly of the Department of Archaeology of Bristol University, also 'tentatively' suggests that it is Romanesque. Some suggest it is 'very, very old' whilst others think the head is of the fourteenth century, and a woman!

At this point in time, the keepers of the head are being very unforthcoming in allowing further investigations into the artefact.

The head has currently been removed from public view, although at some point in the near future it is to be secured in an elevated position in the church. Unfortunately this will prevent proper inspection of it, and also prevent, or at least make more difficult, further academic investigations to be carried out.

Gazetteer

1086: The lands of the Bishop of Coutances consisted of:

> 2 thanes held it before 1066; it paid tax for 9 hides and ½ virgate of land. Land for 9 ploughs. In lordship 3 ploughs; 13 slaves; 4 hides and 3 virgates.

The Cameley Head. (Courtesy of Andy Sims)

*The back of the Cameley
Head, carved into nine squares.
(Courtesy of Andy Sims)*

9 villagers; 1 smallholder and 7 cottagers with 4 ploughs & 3 hides &
1½ virgates. A mill which pays 5s; meadow, 120 acres; pasture, 30 acres;
underwood 50 acres. 2 cobs; 12 cattle; 21 pigs; 150 sheep. The value was £7;
now £10. Humphrey holds 1 hide of this manor's land; he has 1 plough there,
in lordship. 3 villagers and 1 cottager with 1 plough. Meadow, 40 acres. 12
cattle; 14 pigs; 70 sheep. Value 20s.

The lands of the Bishop of Coutances were later held by the Barony of
Trowbridge or the Earls of Lincoln and of Gloucester.

1135–54: The first mention is made of de Mariscos in connection with the
Isle of Lundy.[2]

1153 (1150?): Alexander de Alneto, his brothers and their mother gave the
manor of Cameley and 70 silver marks to the monks of St Peter's at Bath.
The grant was confirmed by William, Earl of Gloucester. According to
the Bath Chartulary, the Alnetos then rented the manor from the monks.[3]
A charter of Henry, Duke of Normandy also mentions this.[4]

As well as the manor, the monks presumably acquired the church. This is
recorded as being in their hands by the end of the century.[5]

Collinson states that 'It is not easy to reconcile this grant of the manor
with the other accounts of it, which for a length of time after the above date
assign its possession to the family de Marisco, who intermarried with the
above-mentioned de Alnetos, Dannos, or Dandos'.[6]

The Cameley Head. (Courtesy of Alex Meadows)

1155: Cameley is recorded as being the dower of William de Marisco's wife, Lucie de Alneto, who is buried with their son Jordan and grandson William in Bath Abbey.[7]

Henry II commanded the return of all lands that had been granted away during his predecessor's reign. These included the Isle of Lundy, which he had granted to the Templars. Henry II made several gifts to the Knights Templars. The de Mariscos failed to comply and remained in possession of the island.[8]

1166: Records state that Geoffrey de Marisco held half a fee of Warin de Aula, then lord of Huntspill.[9]

1175–88: (Possibly before August 1179) The *English Episcopal Acta Bath & Wells* contains the following extracts:

> Inspeximus and confirmation of Alexander de Alneto's grant to the monks of Bath of the church of Long Ashton, made in recompense for the injury, which he did them in the manor of Cameley.[10]

> Inspeximus and confirmation of Alexander de Alneto's grant to the monks of Bath of the church of Cameley and half a mark from the mill of Cameley, and of his promise that on his death his body is to be buried at Bath.[11]

One of the witnesses to this charter is Asketillo de Chywton.

1189: *July–December:* A charter of 'Richard King of England, Duke of Normandy and Aquitaine, Count of Anjou' confirms the grants to the Knights Templars made in previous reigns, including the Island of Lundy.[12] (The grant of the Isle of Lundy to the Templars is usually attributed to John.)

1194–5: The Pipe Rolls record that William de Marisco owed 300 marks for retaining custody of Lundy.[13] For his rebellion, de Marisco was to be outlawed.[14]

1197: William de Marisco is recorded as fighting for the King in France.[15]

1199–1200: A charter of King John confirms that the Island of Lundy belongs to the Templars.[16] King John also made a confirmation of the Templars' privileges, but they had to pay £1,000 for this right.[17]

1200: The de Mariscos retained their hold on the Island of Lundy. 'In or before 1200' William de Marisco (Marsh) pledged his manor of Huntspill to guarantee his gift of the island to the Templars. The manor was evidently not handed over.[18] This only mentions Huntspill; there is no mention of Cameley.

1201: The Pipe Rolls state that William de Marisco owed 120 marks for holding the Isle of 'Ely' [*sic*].[19] The Oblate Rolls state that:

> The Templars owe 50 marks and a palfrey for having lands in Somerset, which were the wages of Nicholas de Kiville as long as William de Marisco shall hold the island of Lunde [sic] against the King's will and theirs.[20]

The Pipe Rolls consistently refer to the Island of Ely, not Lundy. This is an oblique reference to Cameley because of the reference to Nicholas de Kiville. (*See* next entry.)

1201–2: The Somersetshire Fines include the following:

> Grant and concord between Nicol de Kivilly, claimant and Henneri Seinte More, magister, tenant, by Brother Robert de Denton in his place; for all the land of William de Marisco in Hunespill and all the vill of Cameleg with appurtenances which Nicol claimed from William de Marisco and by the confirmation of the King. Henneri conceded to Nicol and his heirs the lands in Huntspill and Cameley, to be held of him, by the farm of ten pounds per annum … until the brothers of the Knights Templars or their successors shall recover the island of Lundy which William de Marisco holds. When the said brethren shall recover the said island, the said Nicol and his heirs shall be quit of the said farm rent, and the land in Hunespill and vill of Cameleg shall remain to him or his heirs quit of the aforesaid brothers and their successors for ever. Nicol quit claimed to Henneri and the brothers of the Knights Templars 42 marks, which he demanded from them.[21]

'Henneri' (Magister of the Templars) would seem to be a misreading as Aymeric of St Maur (or Mawr) was Master of Knights Templars in England 1200–18, the period from which this document dates. Aymeric can sometimes be represented as Emmeri (eg in the Curia Regis Rolls), this is not so very different from Henneri, therefore it is possible that this may have been an error in the original document or there could have been an error in transcription.

The vill of Cameley had come to William de Marisco as the dower of his wife Lucie de Alneto.

Nicol de Kivilly was a sub-tenant of the de Mariscos, but by this concord became, at least for the time being, a tenant of the Templars, this was only supposed to be a temporary arrangement. De Kivilly may also be rendered as Knovill.

1202: The Pipe Rolls state that William de Marisco owed 120 marks for holding the Isle of 'Ely' [*sic*],[22] that 'the sheriff [of Devon] makes a return of 40 marks, which he had received for defence of the ports against William de Marisco' and that the Templars 'ought to have seisin of their Island whence they were disseised unjustly'.[23]

1204: The Pipe Rolls again list that William de Marisco owed 120 marks for holding the Isle of 'Ely' [*sic*].[24] The King grants de Marisco the manor of Braunton.[25] De Marisco was also appointed to the command of some of the royal galleys.

The King's quarrel with the Church may have adversely affected the Templars' position as an order of 1204 granted to 'the Brethren of the Temple to have yearly at the Exchequer £10 granted to them until the King shall have assigned to them £10 worth of land, or until they have right against William de Marisco of the Isle of Lunde'. [26]

Ralph of St Maur brought a case of Novel Disseisin against William de Marisco. Ralph accused de Marisco of disseising him of his free tenement in Cloud. The jurors ruled that Ralph had his seisin and William de Marisco was fined 20*s*. Reference is made to 'those lands of William de Marisco then in the hands of the Lord King caused by the outlawing of the same William'.[27] Is this related in some way to the Templars obtaining Cameley as compensation for the Island of Lundy from William de Marisco? When he was outlawed his lands were in the hands of the King. Had Ralph of St Maur been somehow involved in this?

1205: William de Marisco still owes 120 marks for holding Lundy.[28]

An Attain of Jury was brought before the Sheriff, Robert de Berkeley and Robert de Ropesle regarding the case of Novel Disseisin between William de Marisco and Ralph of St Maur concerning land in Cloud. The jury of twelve admitting to swaring falsely that Ralph had never had seisin of the land in question. (Ralph had been given a charter(s) when Anketil was on his death bed, then he went before the hundred court of Chewton?). Afterwards, he went to Cloud, broke the door of the dovecots, took doves, and then, he went into the garden and took apples. The jurors would seem to have been Albert of Easton; Simon Cook? (quoque) of Pateshull; Osbert of Esces; Richard of Bikefaud; Joceline of Stoke; William Beket; Geoffrey of Stanton; Jordan Blundell; Stephen of Edweie, William Cole; and Walter Malreward (only eleven names are given).[29]

1206: William de Marisco still owes 120 marks for holding Lundy.[30]

1207: William de Marisco owes 108 marks.[31]

1208: William de Marisco owes 108 marks.[32]

1209: William de Marisco owes £53 7s 4d.[33]

1210: William de Marisco owes £43 7s 4d.[34]

1211: William de Marisco owes £22 8s.[35]

1216: William de Marisco was probably one of the English barons who sided with Louis, son of the King of France against King John.[36] William de Marisco was declared an outlaw and his lands were ordered to be confiscated.[37]

1217: In July of this year William de Marisco was one of the prisoners captured by the English after a naval battle with the French fleet bringing reinforcements to Louis of France, off the town of Sandwich. The shipping was provided by Eustace the Monk, a pirate. Eustace was captured and executed after the battle.[38]

Henry III succeeded to the throne. On 17 September, peace was concluded and all prisoners were absolved and freed. On 7 November, Hugh de Vivonne was advised 'Know that William de Marisco has satisfied us as to his loyalty and therefore we bid you restore, without any delay, the Island of Lundy, belonging to the aforesaid William, and William's wife with his four sons and two daughters captured on the island'.[39]

1219: William de Marisco was charged £11 4s for retaining possession of Lundy.[40]

1220: William de Marisco was still in occupation of Lundy, but the Templars were given 100s 'in lieu and full recompense for it'.[41]

1222: William de Marisco was allowed to move to Lundy the mangonels, which he had on his lands at Cameley.[42]

1225: William de Marisco died peacefully.[43] His nephew, also William de Marisco, later turned pirate and managed to hold out on Lundy for seven years until 1242.[44]

1227: In February, in one of his first charters, Henry III confirmed the grants of his father to the Templars, but he omitted to mention the grant of the Island of Lundy. They had been compensated for its loss and Langham states that this 'explains the omission of the island from the charter of 1227'.[45]

The Templars would seem to have held Cameley for only a limited period of time.

There is an undated reference to the croft of Richard de Templo in the Buckland Chartulary no. 92. (*See* below for 'The Hospitaller connection with Cameley'.)

1242–3: De Marisco's connection with Babington is illustrated by two entries in the Somerset Pleas:

> Suit between Robert de Marisco and Walter Page. Robert seeks against Walter Page five ferlings of land with appurtenances in Babington as his right, Robert was seised as of fee and of right during the reign of the present King, with profits to the value of 10*s*. Walter vouches to warranty the Master of the Knights Templars in England. Case to come before the court on the octave of the Purification of the Blessed Mary. Robert is to be represented by Jordan de Marisco.[46]

> Fine levied at Westminster in the quinzaine of Easter. Between Robert de Marisco claimant and Walter Page tenent, for a virgate of land and a quarter. Robert quit claimed to Walter for which Walter gave him 3 marks.[47]

The Curia Regis Rolls also mention him:

> Walter Page gives half a mark pro licencia concordandi cum Robert de Marisco de placito terre by the pledge of the same Robert.[48]

1283–4: Collinson states that 'William de Marisco held this manor, and after him Stephen de Marisco, or Marreys'.[49]

1284–5: John de Marisco holds the vill of Cameley by the service of one knight's fee.[50]

1292: The church was valued at 9 marks and a yearly pension of 1 mark was paid out of the parsonage to St Peter's Abbey at Bath.[51]

1303: Herbert de Marisco holds Cameley by the service of one knight's fee from.[52]

1333: Records state that:

> Grant from John le Duc de La Temple to Joce de Bavise lord of Hallatrow (Halghtre) and Margaret his wife of a messuage and curtilage in La Temple in the parish of Cameley, and 2½ acres of land in the fields of Cameley, rendering to the lords of the fee, one grain of pepper and to the said John and his wife 2s of silver for their lives.[53]

John Duke is listed as holding an area called 'La Temple' in Cameley.[54]

ENDNOTES

1. Blair, J., 'A Romanesque timber beak head from Cameley, Somerset' *The Antiquities Journal*, vol. 71 (1991), pp. 252–264
2. Langham, A.F., *The Island of Lundy* (Alan Sutton Publishing, 1994), p. 12
3. Bath Chartulary 67, pp. 123–4
4. Bath Chartulary 68, p. 125
5. J. Blair (1991), p. 258
6. Collinson ii, p. 125
7. Langham (1994), p. 13; he refers to Collinson ii, p. 392
8. Langham (1994), p. 12
9. VCH viii Huntspill
10. Bath Cathedral Priory 59: Ramsey (ed) 'Extracts from English Episcopal Acta Bath & Wells 1061–1205' *OUP*, pp. 48–9
11. ibid, p. 50
12. Charters and Documents General Royal Charters, pp. 140–2
13. Langham (1994), p. 12
14. Powicke, *The Murder of Henry Clement and the Pirates of Lundy Island* (1949), p. 50
15. Langham (1994), p. 12
16. Dugdale, *Monasticon Anglicanum* Vol. vi Part 2 (1830), p. 842; Monasticon Diocesis Exoniensis; Cart Rot I John
17. Hardy, Rot. de Oblat. and Fin, Rec. Com. p. 13; cited in *Houses of Military Orders*: 8. The Temple British History Online
18. VCH vii, Huntspill, p. 98; citing Pipe R. 1200, (PRS NS 12), p. 99; Rot Lib (Rec Com) p. 66; *SRS* vi, pp. 9 10
19. Pipe Roll 3 John, p. 25
20. Oblate Roll 3 John, p. 31
21. Somersetshire Fines Richard I–Edward I, 1892, *SRS* Vol. 6, pp. 8–9
22. Pipe Roll 4 John, p. 86

23. Pipe Roll 1202 cited in Langham (1994), p. 13
24. Pipe Roll 6 John, p. 177
25. Lyson, *Magna Britannia* Vol. 6 (Devonshire) part 2, p. 587, cited in Langham (1994), p. 13
26. Liberate Rolls 2 May 1204 cited in Langham ibid
27. Pipe Rolls 1204; Curia Regis Rolls vol. 3, p. 128
28. Pipe Roll 1205, cited in Langham ibid
29. Pipe Rolls 1205; Curia Regis Rolls Vol. 3, pp. 332–3
30. Pipe Roll 1206, cited in Langham ibid
31. Pipe Roll 1207, cited in Langham ibid
32. Pipe Roll 1208, cited in Langham ibid
33. Pipe Roll 1209, cited in Langham ibid
34. Pipe Roll 1210, cited in Langham ibid
35. Pipe Roll 1211, cited in Langham ibid
36. The Church Historians of England containing the Chronicle of Melrose Revd Joseph Stevenson 1856 Vol. 4 Part 1, pp. 162–9, cited in Langham (1994), p. 13 or 14?
37. Rott Litt Claus (Rec Com) I, p. 250; cited in VCH viii, Huntspill, p. 98
38. Powicke, *The Thirteenth Century 1216–1307* Second Edition (Oxford University Press, 1961), pp. 10, 13
39. Letters Patent 7 November 1217, cited in Langham (1994) p. 13 or 14?
40. Pipe Roll 1219, cited in Langham (1994), p. 14
41. Langham (1994), p. 14, he does not give his source
42. ibid
43. ibid
44. Powicke (1949), p. 51
45. Langham (1994), pp. 49–50
46. Somersetshire Pleas *SRS* Vol. xi, p. 163
47. Somerset Fines *SRS* Vol. vi, p. 112
48. *Habeant Cirographum* Curia Regis Rolls xvii p. 370
49. Collinson ii, p. 125
50. ibid
51. ibid, p. 126, citing *Taxat Spiritual*
52. Inquisitions and Assessments Relating to Feudal Aids prep under the superintendence HC Maxwell Lyte, p. 309
53. Somerset Record Office DD/Hi 48
54. Johanne le Duk, 1327 Lay Subsidy Returns

6

TWO TEMPLAR ESTATES AT HYDON ON THE MENDIP HILLS

The place-name Hydon (spelt Hidun or Hidon in the twelfth century) applies to a broad ridge running north-west to south-east to the north of the Cheddar Head valley, but it has no specific boundaries. Charterhouse Hydon, part of the Witham Carthusian Estate within the Mendip Royal Forest, lies on the western side of the Hydon ridge and shares a boundary with the Templar estates in West Harptree and Blagdon on the eastern side.

Temple Hydon Estate, West Harptree (granted c.1154–72)

Historical background: Twelfth and early thirteenth century
John Fitz Richard, who probably built Harptree Castle (also known as Richmond Castle) on a steep promontory in East Harptree, died around 1120. He was succeeded by his son William Fitz John(I) de Harptree, who was married to Denise de Manderville. He was known as a supporter of Henry I's daughter Maud and her half-brother Robert, Earl of Gloucester; and for possession and loss of Harptree Castle to Stephen in 1138. During Stephen's reign he served Maud's son, the future Henry II, in Normandy, as a constable, during which time he was referred to as 'Lord of Tilly' (Tilly-sur-Seulles, near Bayeux).

After Henry came to the throne, William continued to serve him in England as a travelling justice having been made a baron. In 1166, he held

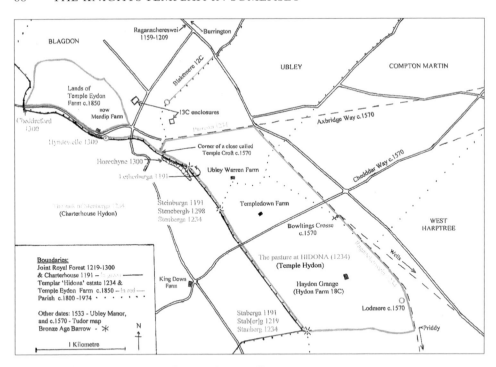

The Templar Estate on Mendip. (Robert Williams)

in chief from the King thirteen and a half fees that were referred to as part of the honour of Bampton. There were two manors in both East and West Harptree, and William Fitz John(I) held one of each parish.

When he died around 1172 his eldest son, Henry de Tilly, who remained in Normandy, initially inherited all his possessions there and in England. However, there was a long-lasting dispute over the inheritance with his younger brother, William Fitz John(II), who was married to Maud Orescuilz. This was eventually settled by King John in Normandy around 1204, with the result that William Fitz John(II) was granted the honour of Harptree and all of its appurtenances, as well as various other possessions in Somerset and also some in Normandy. At that time, William Fitz John(II)'s son and heir, Thomas, was married to Eve de Gournay, and they had a son, Robert. In 1205, the family were honoured by a visit from King John to Harptree Castle.

Thomas Fitz John, who died around 1219, predeceased his father, and also his mother Matilda, who died around 1125. When William Fitz John(II) died in 1231, the inheritance in East and West Harptree and elsewhere passed to Thomas's son Robert. He was also vested in several manors and other possessions in north-east Somerset, together with the considerable possessions elsewhere inherited by his late mother Eve de Gournay, who died around 1230. Robert assumed his mother's family name 'Gournay' (later spelt 'Gurney'), as it was of much higher standing than de Harptree or Fitz John.

The gift and location corrected

The 1185 Survey of Templar lands and possessions in England includes the following entry in a list of appurtenances to Bristol (Temple Fee) in five counties in the South West including Somerset:[1] *'Apud Bissopswrthe. Ex dono Willelmi fillii Iohannis Ix acras quas tenet Edricus et Orgarus pro v. sol'*. This translates as: 'In the neighbourhood of Bishopsworth. By the gift of William son of John, 60 acres, tenant Edric the *Orgarus* who pays rent of five shillings'. Lees noted that Collinson, in *Victoria County History: Somerset, 2*, thought that the entry probably related to Bishopsworth, in Bedminster parish, Somerset, south-west of Bristol (it became a suburb of the city in 1951).

Collinson notes that William Fitz John held unidentified land in Somerset in the twelfth-century.[2] Lees added a note that Edric held Bishopsworth before 1066, but this is inconclusive, as there are no less than twenty pre-conquest landowners named Edric, including the one in the manor of West Harptree later held by William Fitz John(I). Collinson's claim still lingers locally and Smith highlighted a possible Templar connection in the naming of Temple Street in Bedminster and Templeland Road in Withywood, Bishopsworth.[3] However, Earl Temple of Stowe owned land at these locations in 1896.[4]

The 1308 Survey of Templar lands and tenements in England is a badly damaged document preserved in The National Archives.[5] The nine entries relating to the county of Somerset have been transcribed by Clive Wilkins and include the following: 'One messuage, one caricate of land, 25 shillings and 4 pence rent with appurtenances in Hydon on Mendip in the same county'. The 1338 Survey of Templar holdings in Somerset that had been acquired by the Knights Hospitallers by that date contains the following entry: 'Land and meadow at Hidone 40 shillings rent'.

'The Calendar of all the Charters and Muniments of Templecombe and all other manors to the same in divers counties renewed by William Hulles Brother of the Hospital of St John of Jerusalem in England and Preceptor' (1396/7)[6] includes entries relating to the original gifts of both Temple Hydon estates on Mendip, and identifies the donors. One (No. 80), relating specifically to the Blagdon estate, will be discussed separately, but the following relates to the West Harptree estate: 'No. 82. Charter of William son of John of Harpentr of common of all pasture of *Mendep* that is to say for a thousand sheep and 60 beasts'. The records of the Courts of the Hospitallers at Temple Newbury in Babington[7] includes a rental of 1505 that translates as: 'Templehydon – of William Powton for a capital messuage there leased to him by an agreement made for a term of life, yearly 40s'.

It remains to prove that the gift of the Temple Hydon estate was at the time of the 1185 Survey located in the neighbourhood of Bishopsworth. In the period 1170–83, William son of Robert Fitz Martin, granted to St Augustine's Abbey, Bristol, a messuage in Blagdon, between the land of the monks of Bath and the 'stagnum of Blakemere', and common pasture above the road from Priddy to Burrington.[8] 'Blakemere' could be the stream that follows the boundary between Blagdon and Ubley and feeds ponds in the mining area of the Blackmoor valley. In 1173, the Benedictine monks of Bath, at the instigation of Henry II, elected as their abbot and bishop, Reginald Fitz Jocelin, who was very influential in the diocese and elsewhere until his death in 1191.

In 1189, Richard I granted a charter to Bishop Reginald and his successors, which allowed 'the right of mining lead wherever they could find it on their lands in Somerset'. A further charter to the see was granted by Henry III in 1235, when Jocelin of Wells, Bishop of Bath, was informed that 'by the King's licence he may cause digging at Hidun in the King's forest of Mendip, to seek for a mine of iron and every other kind of mine'. Shortly after, the grant was extended to empower the bishop to not only dig at Hidun but 'elsewhere upon the hill of Mendip in the lands of those from whom he can obtain leave, in search of a mine of lead as well as iron'. Soon after, Bishop Jocelin and his successors were granted rights to extract mineral ores in the same area.[9] It is open to speculation whether the Templars profited by either giving the bishop's permission to dig for lead or other minerals on their lands, or being granted rights to do so themselves. It is clear that at the time of the 1185 Survey, Bishop Reginald held a messuage and common land on Mendip in the same neighbourhood as the two Templar estates.

Misappropriation and recovery of the Templar estate in West Harptree
William Fitz John(I)'s grant of land in West Harptree to the Templars was made between 1154 and his death 1172. It has already been explained how his second son, William Fitz John(II), gained possession of the Honour of Harptree and its appurtenances in about 1204. Sometime between that date and his death in 1231, he is identified as 'William son of William son of John of Harptree' in a charter to St Augustine's Abbey of Bristol, when 'with the assent of his wife he grants in free alms pasturage for 1,000 sheep

and 60 draught animals in West and East Harptree, and in his pasture on Mendip belonging to these manors. He also grants pannage for 20 pigs in his woods of Bukelea at Hoclea and Great Whistley'.[10] These place names now survive as Buckley Wood on Hook's Hill and Great Whistley.

Soon after the death of William Fitz John(II) in 1231, his grandson and successor, Robert de Gournay (also spelt Gurnay or Gurney) was to learn that his grandfather's grant to St Augustine's Abbey, and other land and rights in the Babington and Coleford area of north-east Somerset were disputed by the Knights Templar. Judgment in this dispute in favour of the Templars was recorded as follows:[11]

> At Westminster, on 10 February 1234; between Brother Robert de Sandford, Master of the Knights Templar in England, querent; and Robert de Gurnay, impedient; for twenty acres of land in Harpetry. Plea of warrenty [*sic*] of deed was summoned. Robert [de Gurnay] acknowledged the said land, and also common of pasture on Menedep for one thousand sheep of two years old, and sixty animals, and pasture at Hidona next the park of Stenberga as far as Putrewa which leads into Raganekerweia, and from Raganekerwiea to Stanberg.

The judgement continues with a description of the lands and rights in the Babington and Coleford area which are dealt with in the chapter on Temple Newbury. This description of the recovered Temple Hydon estate in West Harptree is divided into three parts:

1) It is unlikely that the '20 acres of pasture' is associated with pannage for twenty pigs in woods mentioned in the grant to St Augustine's Abbey and it remains unidentified.
2) The 'common of pasture for the 1,000 sheep and 60 animals on Mendip' would be shared with other local parishes or manors with rights of common on Mendip.
3) The 'pasture at Hidona' was an estate with defined boundaries where the Templars were tenants in chief and only answerable to the Pope, freeing them from local diocese control and taxes. The extent of this land is discussed later.

The Temple Hydon Estate, Blagdon (granted *c.* 1154–9)

(Recent research by Barry Lane in 2008 has revealed fresh information about this estate which has been included here with his permission.)

The 1185 Survey of Templar property in England includes the following entry as one of the appurtenances of Bristol, Temple Fee:[12] '*Apud Menedepe. Ex dono Roberti filli Martini, una terre que reddit dimidiam*'. This translates as, 'In the neighbourhood of Mendip. By the gift of Robert son of Martin, land which renders rent of half a mark'.

Robert Fitz Martin was born about 1084. He inherited the barony of several manors including Blagdon from his mother, Geva de Burci, who was daughter of Serlo de Burci, the Domesday Lord of Blagdon. Robert Fitz Martin supported Empress Matilda against Stephen in her cause for the throne, as did many other barons in the South West. He had died by 1159, so his gift to the Templars must have been before then, and probably after Henry II came to the throne in 1154.

The gift is not specifically mentioned in the 1308 Inquest of Templar lands in Somerset and Dorset (translated by Clive Wilkins), but it is postulated that it could be one of the 'appurtenances' in the entry relating to the Templars' West Harptree estate. The Blagdon gift was confirmed by a brief entry in the 'Calendar of all Charters and Muniments of Templecombe ... renewed by the Hospitallers by 1396/7.' Entry No. 80 translates as: 'Charter of Robert son of Martel of five plough lands in Blakedon within Menedep granted to the Templars'. The name of Martel must have been a clerical error for Martin. The records of the Courts of the Hospitallers held at the manorial court of Newbury Temple in Babington,[13] includes the following rental of 1505 that translates as: 'Blakedon – of Thomas Bath for a little tenement of customary land there, four shillings'.

Barry Lane reproduced an 1820 sketch plan of the Revd John Skinner, which shows Mendip Farm as an unnamed building with fields on the hill slopes to the north and east marked 'Temple Hydon'. He also reproduced a map around 1850 showing the fields belonging to 'Temple Eydon Farm', now Mendip Farm. This may not be the original extent of the grant to Templars estate in Blagdon but there cannot be any doubt that it was in this vicinity.

Locating the Templar estates at Hydon

The perambulation of the Forest Bounds on Mendip in 1298[14] provides the following description that helps to confirm the location of both estates. A boundary point of Hyndewelle is generally accepted as a spring at the side of the road close to Mendip Farm, after which the boundary description is translated as 'And proceeding from there between the fee of the Templars and the fee of Charterhouse up to Horechne', which refers to one of the deep mining rakes on the south side of the Blackmoor valley. The 1191 Charterhouse perambulation, which shared the forest boundary in this

The 1191 Charterhouse perambulation, showing the Bronze-Age burial mound Letherburga, cut through by ancient mine workings. (Courtesy of Robert Williams)

The 1234 Templar perambulation, showing Stenburg and Stanberg (on skyline) barrows. (Courtesy of Robert Williams)

area, records a Letherburga, a Bronze-Age burial mound, on the edge of a mining rake that was recorded as 'The Turrett over the Weste Myneries' on the 1570 map.

The 1298 Forest perambulation continued between the fees of the Templars and Charterhouse to the burial mounds of Stenebergh and then Stoburghe[15] where the Forest bounds started and ended. This determines the western edge of 'the pasture of Hidona next the park of Stenburga as far as Putrewa', which is postulated to be a section of Axbridge Way of the 1570s map. This meets Raganekerweia at a crossroad, which in a Blagdon charter 1159 x 1208 is spelt Raganacherswei, and in another charter of the same period is said to be the road between Burrington and Priddy. Walker suggests that the name translates as Rough Acres Way. The continuation of this way from the crossroad southward was abandoned during the late eighteenth-century enclosure period, when the route of the modern road further to the north was chosen. The original route and Bowltings Crosse is shown on the 1570s map, and on a 1777 map it is shown on the boundary of the Temple Hydon estate. It is called 'The Font' and was accurately located abutting a wall junction on the 1791 Compton Martin enclosure map, and recently found to be a large rock with a 5in sq slot on the top.[16] It is postulated that the last leg of the 1234 Templar perambulation to Stanberg follows the modern estate boundary, known to exist in around 1777.

Although in around 1850 the fields of Temple Eydon Farm did not extend into the Blackmoor valley, the 1533 perambulation of Ubley refers to, 'the corner of a close called Temple Croft' suggesting that the two Templar estates did meet at this point (see map). It is pointed out that following the dissolution of the monasteries the Templar estates passed into secular hands and there followed long-lasting disputes over local parish boundaries, which were not finally settled by the local parliamentary enclosure acts in the late eighteenth century. Note also the two banked enclosures with internal ditches; excavation of one revealed the foundations of a rectangular building and thirteenth-century pottery. It is suggested that these were possibly stock enclosures with a shelter in areas of common grazing, which may only have been used seasonally.

ENDNOTES

1. Lees (1935), p. 62
2. Pipe Rolls 12 & 14 Henry II
3. Smith (2002), p. 120
4. Smyth estate map, Bristol Record Office

5. TNA E142/111,008
6. Winchester College Muniment 12843, and Harvey, J.H., 'Templar Holdings in East Somerset', *Somerset and Dorset Notes & Queries* Vol. 31 (1980), p. 71
7. Winchester College Muniment, 12864, and ibid, p. 138
8. Walker, D. (ed) *The Cartulary of St Augustine's Abbey, Bristol.* Gloucestershire Record Series, Vol. 2, (Bristol and Gloucestershire Archaeological Society, 1998), pp. 218-219
9. Gough, J.W., *The Mines of Mendip*, Second Edition (David Charles Newton Abbott, 1967), pp. 49–51
10. Walker (1998), pp. 210–211
11. Green, E. (ed), 'Feet of Fines for the County of Somerset, Richard I to Edward I' *Somerset Record Society*, Vol. 6 (1892), pp. 77–78
12. Lees (1935), p. 61
13. Winchester College Muniment 12864
14. Gough (1930), p. 181
15. cf. Stab[er]g 1219, Stanberg 1234, Walker, 1998, pp. 218–219
16. Williams, 2007

7

SMALLER TEMPLAR HOLDINGS IN SOMERSET

Lopen

Lopen originally formed part of the Saxon Royal estate of South Petherton, although its history stretches back long before that time to the Roman period and doubtless earlier. In 1086, the village, that was spelt Lopen or Lopene (meaning Lufa's pen or fold), comprised three Domesday settlements. Lopen Mill was in use at Domesday.

The Templar possessions at Lopen are not mentioned in the 1185 Inquest of Templar lands, but by 1240 Lopen Farm estate had been granted to them by Miles de Fraunchenney (alternatively given as Franco Querco or Franckensi).

The mosaic

In 2001, workmen working near Mill Farm made a remarkable discovery. They inadvertently uncovered the remains of a Roman mosaic dating back 1,640 years! The mosaic consisted of red, blue and white tiles and had clearly formed part of the floor of a Roman villa. It has been suggested by some experts that further mosaics may still be hidden beneath the field. The mosaic has been re-covered in turf to protect it, but a copy remains for visitors to see on part of the floor in Lopen church.

Lopen lies close to the Fosse Way, a major Roman road that was later used by the Templars as it lay close to their preceptory at Templecombe.

Lopen Farm

Lopen Farm, which has now been renamed Manor Farm, was the centre of the Templar estate, the ground plan of the present farm may reflect that of an earlier building and could represent the ruined messuage that is mentioned in documents from around 1312 and 1338. It is probable that this estate, which became known as Temple Lopen, corresponds with one of the three Domesday settlements, and was formerly an area of earlier Anglo-Saxon occupation. The Templar estate was the largest one in the parish and earthworks that exist today to the north of Frog Street may represent the site of former dwellings on the Templar estate.

The gift of Miles de Fraunchenney to the Templars consisted of '1 hide of land with appurtances'. The later 1338 Hospitaller survey speaks of a 'ruined messuage', or manor house, 89 acres of land, 10 acres of meadow and pasture for 100 sheep. This is evidence, yet again, that the former templar lands and property had fallen into disrepair after their suppression and before the Hospitallers had inherited them.

Lopen Fair

By 1201, the King had given permission for a fair which was held at Lopen at the spot known as the Cross Tree, and the remains of the medieval cross shaft is still to be found there. The Cross Tree Joinery, which is built close to the place where the fair was once held, today has a sign bearing a gold Templar cross, a fitting reminder of how things once were.

It is reputed that a young Cardinal Wolsey having visited the fair here became so drunk that he was put in the stocks by the lord of the manor – evidently Somerset cider had the same effect then as it does today!

A medieval seal

In recent times a medieval seal was discovered in the garden of a cottage near the church, identified by archaeologist Nick Griffiths, it is thought to be twelfth century. The seal is made from a copper alloy, possibly bronze and is about 2cm in diameter.

The seal bears the image of a kneeling figure that is believed to depict either a monk or priest. It is hard to identify whether the figure has a monk's tonsure or not. If the seal has any connection with the Knights Templar then no tonsure would be evident because the Templars wore their hair cropped short, or at least not very long and they frequently wore a beard. The image on the seal also shows three dots beneath the hands of the kneeling figure, which may represent a portable altar, there is also a star and an inscription around the edge reading 'I believe in my God'.

Templar Cross at the Cross Tree Joinery, Lopen. (Courtesy of Robert Williams)

Long Load

It was sometime between 1154 and 1184 that the lord of the manor of Martock, Pharamus of Boulogne granted the Knights Templar land in 'Lade', which later became known as Long Load. The word 'lade' means watercourse. Pharamus of Boulogne is described in the 1185 Inquest as 'frater' (brother); it is suggested that he joined the Order later in life, as he is not styled frater at the time of his earlier grants.

The village of Long Load comprises a long street running from Martock to the medieval Load Bridge, which crosses the River Yeo or Ivel and is a navigable river. In 1379, a bridge house was situated to the south of the bridge, and in later times remains of wharves and staves were found and documented. Clearly the river was of extreme importance to the inhabitants of the village both as a means of access and a food souce. Navigable waterways would have been utilized by the Templars, and probably provided a safer form of transport than road where there was the constant risk of highway robbers or outlaws.

The Monks' Seal, front view.
(Courtesy of Mr and Mrs Hider)

The Monks' Seal, back view.
(Courtesy of Mr and Mrs Hider)

In the 1338 Hospitaller Survey, a 'ruined messuage' is mentioned. This probably represented the Templar manor house. In 1327, a chapel was in existence that may have been associated with the Templars at an earlier time; unfortunately it has been completely demolished.

Today there are still visible earthworks to the south of the village which are of archaeological interest, including boundaries, house platforms and what are believed to be the remains of fish ponds.

Worle

In 1256, William de Stures granted to the Templars 'all the lands and tenements with a capital messuage and all the parcels of land which the said [William] acquired'. This gift led to a case of 'unlawful disseisin' and went before a judge Sir Henry of Bracton. The case was brought by the Master of the Knights Templar against William de Stures of Worle because William claimed he was forced by the Templars to part with his land. William stated that whilst he was staying at the Templar manor of Combe, the Templars 'forced his seal from him and what charter they wished whilst he was helpless to resist them'.

Unfortunately for William, the judge, Sir Henry of Bracton, did not believe his story and found in favour of the Templars, and William lost his land!

Doulting

A document drawn up after the court with view of Frankpledge, held at Temple Newbury on 4 November 1505, refers to a tenement called 'Templerlees' in Doulting, with four closes of pasture and customary land and common pasture. Templerlees probably represents the area around Temple House Farm, at Doulting near Shepton Mallet. It is doubtful whether any features of the Templar period remain in the present farmhouse, although local legend suggests that pilgrims used to stay at the farm *en route* to Glastonbury abbey. So far the story is not backed up by documentary evidence.

Lullington

It is indicated in the 1505 rental of the Knights Hospitaller, that the Knights Templar held lands at Lullington. Little information has been discovered concerning this. It is interesting to note however that hidden in the vestry of the Romanesque church at Lullington is an unusual cross slab grave cover. The design on it shows a Templar cross set upon a plinth, with a hand of God (*Dextra Dei*) pointing downwards through the clouds as if in blessing. Clearly the slab is very early, and the grave must have contained the body of someone important to have such a carving on the front. Whether this could have been a Templar Knight as the cross suggests, or whether it was someone who had connections with the Order will probably remain unknown.

An ancient grave slab with a Templar cross on it, Lullington. (Courtesy of Alex Meadows)

Lullington Church. (Courtesy of Alex Meadows)

Crewkerne

The Knights Templars held land and property at Crewkerne, and by 1703 the trustees of the grammar school were using a seal that linked the school with the Holy Trinity Chantry and the Templars, who once held part of the school estate.[1]

ENDNOTES

1.   *VCH* Vol iv, Dunning and Bush, p. 28

8

THE IDOL OF THE TEMPLARS

The Visible image portrays an invisible truth.

Ancient church text 1000

Endless speculation surrounds the 'idol in the form of a head' that the Knights Templar allegedly possessed and were said to have venerated as God. This idol was mentioned time and again at Templar trials, and ultimately those who sought to bring about the downfall of the Order claimed that the 'idol', sometimes referred to as 'Baphomet' or 'Yalla', represented something dark and heretical. That the Templars were very secretive, and they often held initiation ceremonies and meetings after dark, or in the early hours of the morning, all added fuel to the inquisitors' fire.

To many of their contemporaries, the Knights Templar were heroes. The Templars epitomized many of the ideals held most dear in the Middle Ages, particularly their religious zeal and military prowess. They were Knights of Christ, who served God in their everyday lives, and fought in battle with legendary courage for their beliefs. However, although they commanded admiration and respect from most, there were others who were jealous and resentful of their power and privilege. There is no doubt that the entire circumstances of the Templars' arrest, imprisonment, trial and suppression, were based on greed, jealousy, a desire for power, and as far as 'the idol' is concerned, a probable misunderstanding of the ceremony and ritual that the Templars conducted.

This chapter examines ideas about the idol that was so frequently mentioned during the Templar trials, and makes possible connections between the Knights and the two unusual images of 'heads' found in Somerset. One head was found at Temple Cloud, the other at Templecombe. Both of these images depict a long-haired man with a forked beard, large staring eyes and long nose. At Templecombe the image takes the form of a panel painting; at Temple Cloud it takes the form of a wooden carving. To understand what these images may represent, and the connection they may have had with the Knights Templar, we must turn to some of the traditions in both the early Christian and pagan world, and to the accounts given about the idol by the Templars at their trial.

The Holy Land at the time of the Crusades would have been a melting-pot of various belief systems and traditions, some evolving from very ancient, pre-Christian ideas. These beliefs would have come together in the Holy Land, and undoubtedly influenced the lives, thoughts and actions of the Crusaders.

One tradition that arose during the religious fervour of the Crusades was a trade in Holy relics, and from one of particular relic arose a 'cult of the Holy Face' that later became known as the Veronica, or true icon (*vera icon*). These images appear to have developed from reverence for the relic that is today known as the Shroud of Turin.

A miraculous image

Edessa was the capital city of Osroerla, otherwise known as the kingdom of Edessa, now modern Turkey. Edessa was the home of the Abdgar dynasty, and early Christianity spread rapidly and became recognised as the official religion of the kingdom. There was a Christian council held at Edessa as early as AD 197, and an amazing cathedral was built there, which was said to be one of the wonders of the ancient world.

By the tenth century, a legend had arisen in Edessa concerning a miraculous image of Christ: It is said that Abgar V, who was suffering from an incurable disease, sent word via a servant to Jesus asking for his healing. Three accounts are given of what supposedly happened in response to this request. One says simply that Jesus wrote to Abgar declining a visit, but saying he would send a disciple, endowed with his power, to help. The second account tells us that Abgar's servant Hannan painted an image of Christ, which on his return he gave to his master, who was miraculously healed, and consequently built a shrine to house the painting. The third account tells us that Christ wiped his face on a towel, and an imprint of his face was left on the towel, which was taken back to Abgar who was miraculously healed.

A similar legend was that of Veronica's Veil, in which Veronica wipes the face of Christ on his way to Calvary, and his blood and sweat leave a miraculous image of his face on her veil.

Whether there is any truth to be found in these stories is debatable. However, from a very early date, historical accounts start to mention a very unusual image of Christ. The image was referred to as 'acheriopoeitos', or 'made without hands', which implied that it had been created by supernatural means, and not painted. This 'face of Christ' was to become known as the Holy Mandylion. Documentary evidence of the unusual relic continued up until the time of the fourth crusade in 1204, it then seems to disappear from all records.

The many historical accounts of this mysterious image of Christ are documented not always as the face described by Abgar, but sometimes as a whole body image on a cloth that had been folded in four, so that only the face was visible. This cloth was frequently referred to as a 'burial cloth'. So were the Mandylion, Veronica's Veil and the relic known today as Turnin Shroud one and the same thing?

Apart from being a miraculous holy relic, the Holy Mandylion was believed to protect the city; consequently the Edessans regarded it as of paramount importance to preserve the sacred cloth. As Christians were still being persecuted at this time, there was a constant risk of it being stolen or destroyed, so it was hidden away behind a stone, high in the city walls from AD 692–5. The stone behind which the Mandylion was hidden was known as the keramion. The hiding of the cloth proved fortuitous, as Edessa was flooded on more than one occasion and the cloth remained unscathed.

The Mandylion at Constantinople

By AD 944 amidst great celebration, the Mandylion, or shroud, was transferred to Constantinople, the capital of Byzantium, for greater protection. Here it is recorded as being housed in the Pharos, or Imperial Treasury, which is famed as having contained the world's most precious Christian relics. In 1203, the crusader Robert de Clari saw in the Church of St Mary of Blanchernae Constantinople, the 'shroud in which Our Lord had been wrapped, which every Friday raised itself upright, so that one could see the figure of Our Lord on it'.

Constantinople was ransacked by the crusaders in 1204, and the precious relics once held in the city were stolen or dispersed. After this time de Clari recalls that he did not see the shroud again, nor did he know what became of it. In 1207, however, Nicholas d'Orrante, Abbot of Casole and papal legate in Athens wrote about relics taken from Constantinople by French knights, and refers to burial cloths. He recalls 'seeing them with our own eyes' in Athens.

From this time onwards no further mention was a made of the Shroud in written history until 1356, when Geoffrey de Charny, the descendant of a notable French knight from the fourth crusade, displayed it at a church at Lirey, in France.

Until recently, those missing years when the Shroud or Mandylion could not be accounted for led many to believe that the Mandylion of Edessa was destroyed and that therefore the Shroud later displayed at Lirey was probably not the same as the Mandylion of Edessa. However, it has been suggested that the Knights Templar had taken the Shroud from Constantinople and secretly kept the precious relic to protect it.

Recently, Barbara Frale, researcher in the Vatican secret archives, appears to have found documentary evidence supporting the idea of the Templars having possession of the Turin Shroud. The document describes the initiation of a French knight, Arnaut Sabbatier, into the Templar Order. He describes being taken to 'a secret place to which only the brothers had access … I was shown a long piece of linen, on which was impressed the figure of a man, and told to worship it, kissing the feet three times'. This description is certainly reminiscent of the garbled confessions that the knights made when under torture, which appears to reveal that it was in fact the image of Christ on the Turin Shroud that they held in deep veneration. The Vatican have recently declared that the Knights Templar were in possession of the Shroud during its missing years.

It has been said that the Templars had an image of the 'Idol' or 'Holy Face' in each of their preceptories. It seems very probable then, that the face on the Shroud emerged in the form of revered icons, or Mandylions, and may well have been the model for the idol that was worshipped at Templar preceptories across Europe. Certainly it is notable that from the time of the appearance of the Mandylion at Edessa a stereotype 'face of Jesus' started to emerge on the many early icons portrayed throughout the East and Europe. These images, sometimes painted faintly on linen cloth, seem to conform to a certain type: a disembodied head of a man with protruding eyes, a prominent nose, forked beard and long hair, the faces were front-facing and usually life size. Another common feature of these icons is that frequently they were displayed in ornate frames or borders featuring a trellis or 'lozenge' design. These frames were often gilded or bejewelled.

Were the 'four idols' that were reputedly brought to England by William de la More for 'safe-keeping' in fact images of the face on the Holy Shroud of Turin?

Two heads in Somerset

In an earlier chapter of this book it was noted that the Knights Templar held the manor of Cameley, and that the Master of the Templars, along with King John, appear to have been patrons of Cameley Church. It could also be argued that the contentious 'Cameley Head' might be linked to the Templars.

As a carbon 14 dating has been unforthcoming, and no formal academic study carried out, we can only surmise as to the origin and purpose of this carving, with the little evidence that is available to us.

It is clear this carved head is very old, and it is thought that it is probably not of European origin. The wood it is carved from has not yet been identified: it is thought not to be oak, which was commonly used in England during the Middle Ages, and some authorities believe that it may be Lebanese cedar. It has been suggested by some that the face on the Cameley Head has Moorish or Semitic features. Certainly it does not appear to be European either in look or design, and is not something one would normally expect to find in a small village church in England.

The lozenge border surrounding the head is reminiscent of the pattern surrounding many icons, suggesting perhaps a Middle Eastern or Byzantine origin for the artefact. In his *Treatise on Decorative Art and Architectural Ornament*, James Ward notes that the Phrygians and Lydians, who inhabited Asia Minor from the eighth century onwards, commonly employed the geometric lozenge motif in their embroidery, and it was to be found decorating the carpets or curtains which hung over the doorways of their homes. In his book *Spiritual Seeing*, Herbert Kessler describes the lozenge motif as representing the Jerusalem veil or curtain, and notes that 'the curtain decorated with lozenges recurs in depictions of the cosmos' in both the Vatican and Sinai manuscripts. It would appear therefore that within iconic tradition, Jesus, through his death and resurrection, is symbolized as parting the veil, to reveal the Mysteries to all who would believe in him. It would seem likely then that the Cameley Head, if it is of Eastern origin, was brought back to England by crusaders (Templars?).

There are several theories that have been put forward regarding the purpose of the head, but one of the predominant ideas is that it may be in the iconic tradition of the Mandylion.

The key arguments for the Cameley Head being in the same tradition as the Mandylion are: that it has the same 'lozenge' border as many icons; it is designed to face the viewer frontally, as are icons, thus inviting contemplation. The features on the Cameley Head bear resemblance not only to the Templecombe panel painting, but also to some of the 'Holy faces' to be found in Europe and the East. One should remember that the Cameley Head would have originally been coloured so would have looked more life-like, and less mask-like than the image we see today.

Art historians have suggested that the lozenge border surrounding the head would originally have been painted in gold, which would imply a very high level of patronage in a tiny village church. This high level of patronage seems to be a recurring theme at Cameley, suggesting perhaps that for some reason the Knights Templar believed the place to be of some significance, either materially (perhaps because of its proximity to their preceptory at Bristol) or spiritually.

At the Templar trials, the knights claimed that the 'heads' they 'worshipped' were made of varying materials, which included some carved in wood. In his book *The Trial of the Templars*, Malcolm Barber describes some of the accounts of the idol, given by the brothers. Brother William of Arreblay states that 'a head made of wood and silver and gilded on the outside' had been brought to chapter meetings and 'the brothers had worshipped this head'. Whilst Brother John Taylafer said that on the day of his reception a 'certain head' had been placed on the altar of the chapel and he was told to adore it. He did not know what substance it was made from, since he had not often gone near it, but it appeared to be the effigy of a human face'. Other Templars gave their own descriptions of a bearded head painted in a beam made of wood.

It seems evident from these accounts that the representations of the head at different preceptories all varied slightly in substance, and appearance, whilst clearly being artistic interpretations of the same thing.

An esoteric tradition
Another theory that has been put forward regarding the Cameley Head is that it emerged from an esoteric tradition. One rather unusual feature is that the reverse of the artefact is carved entirely into nine inverted pyramids. The original purpose of these is unknown to us, but in the esoteric tradition the number nine was of great numerological and symbolic importance. If the head is of eleventh–thirteenth century in origin, and comes from the Middle East, this would have allowed contact with the esoteric traditions of Judaism, Islam, Greece and Rome and also possible remnants of Babylonian lore. It has been suggested that the nine inverted pyramids may

represent the square of the planet Saturn, and that precious stones, relics or small scrolls with prayers written on them were originally placed within each hollow. During the Middle Ages there was complex symbolism of the seven planets. One aspect of this was that the planets are manifestations in the physical world of higher, cosmic forces. If this is the case, then the Cameley Head was probably some form of talisman, and could be 'read' and understood by those with the necessary knowledge and understanding.

The entire subject is far too complex to discuss in detail here, but does offer an intriguing possibility as to the origins of the mysterious Cameley Head!

Whichever tradition they may have emerged from, and whether or not they had anything to do with the Knights Templar, it seems that the two heads discovered in Somerset may have served a similar purpose; they probably served as a 'pictorial narratives'. In the tradition of icons, every detail of the making and presenting of the image was touched with prayer and contemplation; icons were not painted, they were 'written'. The resulting image was a 'window to heaven' enabling the viewer to transcend this word and be transported 'beyond the veil' in divine meditation.

In his book *Spiritual Seeing*, Herbert Kessler suggests that artistic Christian images served as intermediaries between human and divine, and they were situated between the spiritual and physical worlds. They were used and understood in a way that is now largely forgotten.

The Templecombe panel

The Templecombe panel painting also appears to represent what is believed to be the head of Christ set within a type of lozenge. When it was originally discovered, the painting had golden stars surrounding it, suggesting a link with the heavenly and eternal realms. It was also once painted in vivid colours that played an important part in iconic symbolism. For example: gold = heavens radiance, red = divine life, blue = human life and so on. These features would seem to suggest that it was an image used for contemplation and devotion.

In the earlier chapter on Templecombe it was mentioned that the panel was found secreted away in the ceiling of an 'outhouse' in part of the cottage where Molly Drew, the painting's discoverer, lived. She described it as a small room attached to her cottage, its only window being a stone 'porthole'. The room would have been able to hold about ten people. According to Audrey Dymock Herdsman, the cottage was once known as

The Templecombe panel painting. (Courtesy of Alex Meadows)

the 'Priests House'. This offers intriguing possibilities as to what the origins of the 'outhouse' may have been. Possibly it was a small chapel where the Templars went to meditate upon the image if the Lord, or even an Initiatory Chapel.

The painting was obviously deliberately hidden at some time, presumably for its protection. This may have been at the suppression of the Templars, or during the Reformation.

It has been brought to my attention recently, that even when this, or other venerated objects were hidden from those who sought their destruction, the place where they were hidden was believed to still retain the power and sanctity of the image or object, and could still be used for secret devotion.

How long could the Templecombe 'outhouse' have continued to be used in this way, before it was forgotten, and became a wood store, which was finally demolished, concealing its secret for all time?

It is surely miraculous that the panel painting survived to hint at its mysterious past.

The Knights of Christ

The latest evidence from the Vatican linking the Templars with the Holy Shroud of Turin, is surely evidence that the Knights Templar were not engaged in malpractice, or worship of idols. Certainly they had been influenced by the learning and traditions of the peoples they had come across whilst in the Holy Land. They had encountered new concepts in architecture, geometry, numerology, music, medicine and industry, and had assimilated ideas from different religions and cultures. On returning home, some of these ideas and practices may have seemed strange or even frightening to their contemporaries in England and Europe. The ceremonies and rituals that the Templars undertook in secret, or after dark, fuelled damaging rumours about their activities.

However, it would appear that many of the higher members of the Order of the Temple were guarding and protecting the Turin Shroud, an object still revered by the Catholic Church. It appears that they were also adhering to an ancient form of Christian mystical adoration, performed during their 'secret' chapters and initiation ceremonies, some of which would have been conducted at their preceptories in Somerset; but they remained true to their vows, and their God … For they believed they had in their possession the Holiest of all relics, which they guarded with their lives, and were prepared to die for: They believed they had the true likeness of Christ Himself.

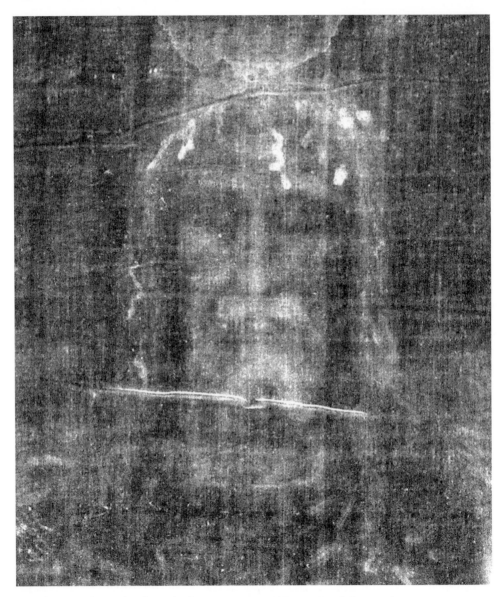

The face on the Holy Shroud of Turin. (© 1978 Barrie M. Schwortz)

And thus did the Knights of the Temple vanish with their secret, in whose shadow breathed a lofty yearning for the earthly city. But the Abstract to which their efforts aspired lived on, unattainable, in unknown regions ... and its inspiration, more than once in the course of time has filled those spirits capable of receiving it.

(Victor Emile Michelet, *Le Secret de la Chevalerie*, 1930)

BIBLIOGRAPHY

BOOKS

Barber, Malcolm, *The Trial of the Templars* Second Edition (Cambridge 2006)

Barber, Malcolm, *The New Knighthood* (Cambridge, 1995)

Baigent, M., Leigh, R. and Lincoln, H., *The Holy Blood and the Holy Grail* (Century 2005)

Brighton, Simon, *In Search of the Knights Templar* (Weidenfeld & Nicholson, 2007)

Charpentier, John, *Les Grands Templiers* (Fasquelle Editeurs, 1935)

Collinson, John, *The History and Antiquities of the County of Somerset* (1791)

Colton, Trish and Holloway, Diane, *The Knights Templar in Yorkshire* (Sutton, 2008)

Cupitt, Don and Armstrong, Peter, *Who was Jesus?* (BBC Publishing, 1977)

Currer-Briggs, Noel, *The Holy Grail and the Shroud of Christ* (ARA Publications, 1984)

Dugdale, William, *Monasticon Anglicanum* Vol. vi Part 2 (1830)

Ellison, Ann, *Medieval Villages in South East Somerset* (Western Archaeological Trust)

Fideler, David, *Jesus Christ Sun of God* (Quest Books; The Theosophical Publishing House, Wheaton, Illinois, 1993)

Frale, Barbara, *The Templars: The Secret History Revealed* (Maverick, 2009)

Gough, J.W., *The Mines of Mendip*, Second Edition (David Charles Newton Abbott, 1967)

Hindle, Paul, *Medieval Roads and Tracks* (Shire, 2009)

Jenkins, Simon, *England's Thousand Best Churches* (Penguin, 2000)

Kessler, Herbert L. *Spiritual Seeing – Picturing God's Invisibility in Medieval Art* (University of Pennsylvania Press, 1999)

Knowles D. and Hadcock, R.N., *Medieval Religious Houses, England and Wales* (Longman, London, 1974)

Langham, A.F., *The Island of Lundy* (Sutton Publishing, 1994)

Laidler, Keith, *The Head of God* (Weidenfeld and Nicholson, 1998)

Lea-Jones, Julian, *Bristol Curiosities* (Birlinn Publications, 2007)

Lees, Beatrice A., *Records of The Templars in England in the Twelfth Century Inquest of 1185* (London 1935)

Lord, Evelyn, *The Knights Templar in Britain* (Longman, 2002)

Martin, Edward J., *The Trial of the Templars* (Allen & Unwin Ltd, 1928)

Newman, Paul, *Somerset Villages* (R. Hale Publications, London, 1986)

Nicholson, Helen, *Knight Templar,* (Osprey; Oxford, 2004)

Parker, T.W., *The Knights Templar in England* (Arizona)

Partner, Peter, *The Murdered Magicians* (Crucible; Oxford, 1987)

Perkins, Clarence, *The Knights Templar in the British Isles* (English Historical Review, 1909)

Powicke, 'The Murder of Henry Clement and the Pirates of Lundy Island', *The Ways of Medieval Life and Thought* (Biblio & Tannen 1949)

Powicke, *The Thirteenth Century 1216–1307* Second Edition (Oxford University Press, 1961)

Ramsey (ed) *Extracts from English Episcopal Acta Bath & Wells 1061–1205* (OUP, 1995)

Read, Piers Paul, *The Templars* (Orion 1994)

Robinson, John J., *Dungeon, Fire and Sword* (Michael O'Mara Books Ltd, 1994)

Simon, Edith, *The Piebald Standard* (Cassell, London)

Smith, V. *The Street Names of Bristol*, Second edition (Broadcast Books; Bristol, 2002)

Tapper, Audrey, *The Knights Templar and Hospitaller in Herefordshire* (Logaston Press 2005)

Tull, George F., *The Traces of the Templars* (The Kings England Press, 2000)

Walker, D. (ed) *The Cartulary of St Augustine's Abbey, Bristol.* Gloucestershire Record Series, Vol. 2, (Bristol and Gloucestershire Archaeological Society, 1998)

Ward, James, *Treatise on Decorative Art and Architectural Ornament,* (Chapman & Hall; London, 1900, 1897)

Whitfield, Mary, *In Praise of Bratton St Maur* (Bratton Publishing, 1974)

Wilkins, David, *Concilia Magnae Britanniae et Hiberniae* (1737)

Williams, Robert G.J., *The Stratford Lane Roman Road and Other Early Routes on Mendip,* (Proceedings of the University of Bristol Speleological Society, 1992)

Wilson, Ian, *The Blood and the Shroud* (Weidenfeld and Nicholson, 1998)

Wilson, Ian, *Holy Faces, Secret Places* (Corgi, 1992)

Wilson, Ian, *Jesus: The Evidence* (Orion, 1998)

JOURNALS & ARCHAEOLOGICAL REPORTS

Anthroposophical Quarterly, Summer, 1960 (The Standard Press; Montrose, Ltd)

'Archaeological Excavations at Templecombe, 1995' *Somerset Archaeological and Natural History Society* (2003)

Blair, J., 'A Romanesque timber beak head from Cameley, Somerset', *The Antiquaries Journal, SANHS*, Vol. 71 (1991)

Dymock-Herdsman, Audrey, *Abbas and Templecombe* (Information sheet, Templecombe Church)

Good, G.L., *Excavation at Water Lane, by Temple Church Bristol 1971* (Published by Bristol and Avon Archaeology, 1992)

Gough, J.W., 'Mendip Mines and Forest Bounds', *Somerset Record Society*, Vol. 45 (1930)

Green, E. (ed), 'Feet of Fines for the County of Somerset, Richard I to Edward I' *Somerset Record Society*, Vol. 6 (1892)

Harvey, J.H., 'Templar Holdings in East Somerset', *Somerset and Dorset Notes & Queries* Vol. 31 (1980) (Two related notes in Vol. 21).

Hugo, 'Mynchin Buckland Priory and Preceptory', *SANHS* 10 (ii) (1860)

Larking, L.B. (ed) 'The Knights Hospitallers in England, being a Report of Prior Philip de Thame to the Grand Master Elyan de Villanova for AD 1338', *Camden Society*, Vol. 65 (1857)

Lopen Church Guide (reprinted 1998)

Taylor, Tim, *Time Team the Site Reports – Templecombe* (Channel 4 Television) *Somerset and Dorset Notes and Queries* Vol. V, Part XXXIV (June, 1896)

Williams, R.G.J. 'The Stratford Lane Roman Road and other early routes on Mendip', *Proceedings of the University of Bristol Speleological Society* Vol. 19(2) (1992)

Williams, Bruce, 'Excavations in the Medieval Suburbs of Bristol', *Bristol and Region Archaeological Srvices* (Published by Bristol City Museum and Art Gallery, 1984)

PRIMARY SOURCES (MANUSCRIPTS)

Documents relating to Templar Holdings in Somerset before 1312, and Hospitaller Holdings in Somerset until the Dissolution (Winchester College Archives)

E142/111 *Dorset and Somerset* (National Archives Public Record Office)

PRIMARY SOURCES (PRINTED)

Calendar of the Fine Rolls
Pipe Rolls
Curia Regis Rolls
(Details and dates of each of these primary sources are given in gazetteer and endnotes at the end of each chapter)

ONLINE ARTICLES

MacLennan, Bruce. Evolution, Jung and Theurgy: v.Theurgy, *www.cs.utk. edu/~mclennan/papers/EJT/VB.html*

Hoggard, Brian, 'Knights of the Temple (Part 1)', *www ~whitedragon.org.*

Lane, Barry (forthcoming), *The Knights Templars in Blagdon.* A History of Blagdon Series, Blagdon Local History Society. A draft of 8/3/08 on-line www. britarch.ac.uk/cat/uploads/CharterhouseEvironsResearchTeam

Living in Jersey-History and Heritage- Eustace the Monk *www.thisisjersey.com/ code/community/history-heritage/*

Other local titles published by The History Press

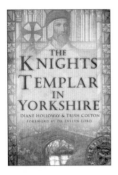

The Knights Templar in Yorkshire
TRISH COTTON & DIANE HOLLOWAY

This book explores what life was like during the Templars' stay in Yorkshire in the Middle Ages. This volume takes the reader on a tour of the ten major Templar sites established in Yorkshire, and reveals what life was like for their inhabitants – how the land was farmed, what the population ate, how they were taxed and local legends.

978 0 7509 5087 9

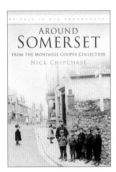

Around Somerset: From the Montague Cooper Collection
NICK CHIPCHASE

Montague Cooper was probably Somerset's first commercial photographer, with studios in Taunton, Burnham and Chard. Although his business was primarily portraiture, he also recorded towns and villages and dozens of events, from fêtes and festivals to railway disasters. Nick Chipchase presents here a fascinating album of his work – a true reminder of bygone days which will appeal to everyone interested in the history of Somerset and the early days of photography.

978 0 7509 4677 3

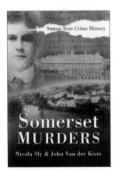

Somerset Murders
JOHN VAN DER KISTE

Somerset Murders brings together numerous murderous tales that shocked the county and made headlines throughout the nation. They include the cases of Elizabeth and Betty Branch, a mother and daughter who beat a young servant girl to death in Hemington in 1740; 13-year-old Betty Trump, whose throat was cut whilst walking home at Buckland St Mary in 1823; and factory worker Joan Turner, battered to death in Chard in 1829. This chilling book will appeal to everyone interested in the shady side of Somerset's history.

978 0 7509 4795 4

The Knights Templar on Trial
HELEN J. NICHOLSON

Although outsiders told stories of abominable Templar rituals, secret meetings and murders at the dead of night, all these tales turned out to be mere rumour. This book is based on extensive research into the records of the trial and other unpublished medieval documents recording their arrest, imprisonment and surveys of their property. It also shows how, by judicious selection of material, the inquisitors made the scanty evidence against the Templars appear convincing.

978 0 7509 4681 0

Visit our website and discover thousands of other History Press books. **www.thehistorypress.co.uk**